AN INTRODUCTION TO CHRISTIAN MINISTRY

*For Lay and Clergy Persons
In the Cumberland Presbyterian Church*

By Morris Pepper

AN INTRODUCTION TO CHRISTIAN MINISTRY: For Lay and Clergy Persons in the Cumberland Presbyterian Church by Morris Pepper. Edited by D. Mark Brown and James W. Knight. Cover design by Matthew H. Gore. Entire contents ©2012 by the Discipleship Ministry Team of the Ministry Council of the Cumberland Presbyterian Church. Published by the Discipleship Ministry Team of the Ministry Council of the Cumberland Presbyterian Church. Distributed exclusively by Cumberland Presbyterian Resources, 8207 Traditional Place, Cordova (Memphis), Tennessee, 38016.

World rights reserved. This book may not be reproduced in whole or in part, or transmitted in any form, or by any means electronic, mechanical, photocopying, recording, or others, without written permission from the publisher, except by a reviewer who may quote brief passages in a review.

Fourth Printing, March 2012

ISBN 10: 0615616372
ISBN 13: 978-0615616377

OUR UNITED OUTREACH
Made Possible In Part By Your Tithe To Our United Outreach

Discipleship Ministry Team
8207 Traditional Place
Cordova (Memphis), TN 38016

AN INTRODUCTION TO CHRISTIAN MINISTRY

*For Lay and Clergy Persons
In the
Cumberland Presbyterian Church*

By Morris Pepper

*edited by Mark Brown
and James Knight*

THE MINISTRY AS A WHEEL

Perhaps the best symbol of ministry is a wheel with the spokes extending out from the hub. Each spoke signifies a role of service, the hub being Christ and his work in which we participate. Here is complete unity and symmetry. When the wheel was invented, the human race rolled forward in a great spurt of progress. But nothing in comparison with the innovation of Christ and his ministry of love.

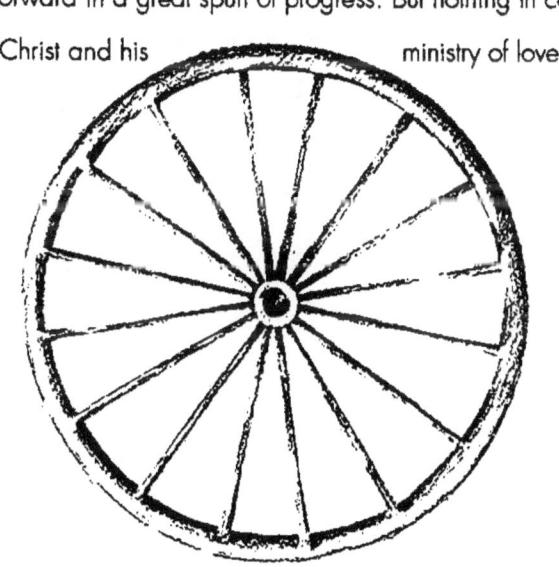

Dedication

To Ruth, who has supported my ministry and been a part of it for fifty-eight years Without forgetting Beverly and John, whose affirmation I have always treasured.

Acknowledgements

My sincere gratitude is hereby expressed to those persons who gave various kinds of help in preparing the manuscript for this publication. These include my wife, Ruth; my daughter, Beverly Brown; the Reverends Norlan Scrudder, James W. Knight, and Mark Brown.

A MANIFESTO

I have nothing to sell. Many people think the minister is a peddler whose commodity is religion. Preaching is making a sales talk. Visiting means cultivating prospects. Evangelism is doing a "hard sell."

I have nothing to sell. Religion is not a commodity. God is not on the counter or in a catalog. God's love and mercy are not Wall Street items. God's blessings will not be found in bargain basements.

I have nothing to sell. I have a witness to make. There are some things which I believe, convictions arising from my thought and life, which I know from within. Of these I witness. They are not mere blessings of tradition. They are real to me because God is real. But they cannot be bought or sold. They can only be witnessed.

I have nothing to sell. I have a message to communicate. It is a story of Jesus Christ, a story of redemption. It is a promise, a promise of what can happen here and now. It is the gospel, the good news of God's love told by one who knows it firsthand. I am a storyteller, a proclaimer, an announcer—not a cocky salesman with a hot line.

I have nothing to sell. I have a friendship to offer. Some are like Job who would like to recapture the days when "the friendship of God was upon my tent." Others have never known such a relationship. Many are afraid of God. Still others are rebellious. To these and others I say, "God loves you. Won't you let God be your friend?"

I have nothing to sell. You can't buy salvation. You can't buy faith. You can't buy heaven. You can't buy God. Nor can you sell them. My job is to offer you an adventure, not to sell you a bill of goods—to invite you to join a mission, not a Cosmos club.

I am not doing hard sell, soft sell, or using psychology. I don't have any tricks to pull out of the bag. So don't raise your sales resistance. I'm an educator, a teacher, a pastor, a counselor—but please, not a huckster! I'm a witness, a communicator, an announcer, a reporter, but never a peddler!

For we are not, like so many, peddlers of God's word; but in Christ we speak as persons of sincerity, as persons sent from God and standing in his presence. (II CORINTHIANS 2:7 RSV AND NRSV)

Morris Pepper in *The Church Spire*, Scottsboro Cumberland Presbyterian Church, Scottsboro, Alabama, revised

Table of Contents

- **4** Introduction
- **5** What is the Christian Ministry?
- **17** The Call to Ministry, With Thoughts on Ordination
- **29** Ministry in the Small Church
- **41** The Pastoral Relationship
- **55** The Pastor as Leader of Worship
- **75** The Pastor as Preacher
- **91** The Pastor as Teacher and Educator
- **103** The Pastor as Evangelist
- **115** The Pastor as Administrator
- **123** The Pastor In Other Roles: Counselor, Theologian, Presbyter, and the Pastor in Relation to the Community
- **139** Epilogue: Symbols of a Unified Ministry

Introduction

This book is an attempt to provide an introduction to Christian ministry. It is intended for both lay and clergy persons in the Cumberland Presbyterian Church. My concept is that Christian ministry is a partnership between them both, with the clergy being responsible for training the laity.

> And his gifts were that some should be apostles, some prophets, some evangelists, some pastors and teachers, to equip the saints for the work of ministry.[1]

My purpose is to write for candidates who are beginning their preparation and those who are in the early stages of their calling. Experienced ministers will have gone beyond the level of this volume.

I have included lay persons because, being partners with the clergy, they need to understand the nature of ministry if they are to serve well.

The word *ministry* suggests service being given *to* and *for* others. It also means serving *with* others. Ministry is a cooperative venture. It must be shared.

Moses' life provides a good example of shared ministry. At the outset of his life he tried to do something *for* his people. He killed an Egyptian who was mistreating a Hebrew. Many years later, he shared his leadership *with* Aaron, Miriam and the people.[2]

Christian ministry is a humble, and humbling, work. We should not do it with an attitude of superiority, as if we have all the answers or can solve all the problems. Rather, it calls us to engage others as equals, with the hope that together we may learn to serve. This concept is a part of our Protestant heritage of the priesthood of all believers.

Many things about Christian ministry will be omitted from this writing. It is designed only as an introduction. I hope this fact will be accepted, and that those who read these pages will use this information as a springboard to greater learning.

Although I have used ideas of my own, and drawn from the treasure of common knowledge, I have also borrowed ideas from many sources. Most of them I remember. Others I have forgotten. I have acknowledged sources insofar as it is possible.

This introduction is an invitation to you to take a journey with me as we search together for better concepts, motivations and ways of doing ministry in the name of Jesus Christ. I hope you enjoy the reading as much as I have the writing.

MORRIS PEPPER, 1992

---

[1] Ephesians 4:11, 12
[2] Exodus 2:11-15; 4:14-17; 18:13-27

 CHAPTER 1

What Is Christian Ministry?

You are either interested or are already engaged to some extent in Christian ministry. It is essential for those who would become Christian ministers to have more than a casual knowledge of their calling. We will consider in this chapter such questions as: What are the major features and elements of Christian ministry? When, why and by whom did it originate? Upon what is it based? Is there a model which can give us a better picture of it?

THE MINISTRY OF JESUS CHRIST

The Christian ministry derives its essential nature directly from the person and work of Christ.[1]

> The essential nature of the Christian ministry has been determined for all time by the ministry of Jesus Christ. All our thinking must take his person and ministry as its starting point...The ministry into which we enter is the ministry of Jesus Christ.[2]

This does not mean we are to copy Jesus' ministry slavishly. It has to be adapted to the needs and conditions of our times. However, the basic pattern and model for our ministry is that of Jesus Christ. We will depart from it only at considerable risk of failure.

In a world of change in which so much of the old has been discarded, it is easy for us to think we must seek novelty and to build our own base for ministry. Dr. James Smart cautions us:

> We are not free to determine its nature as we will; its nature has already been determined for us by his life, death, resurrection and by the work of his Spirit in the shaping of the apostolic ministry.[3]

If it is true, and we assume that it is, then we are ready to ask, "What is the shape and form of Christ's ministry?"

---

[1] *A Biographical Word Book of the Bible*, Alan Richardson, Macmillan, page 146.

[2] *The Rebirth of Ministry*, James D. Smart, Westminster, pp. 18, 20 (out of print).

[3] Ibid. page 20.

A MINISTRY CENTERED IN PEOPLE

Reflect for a few moments on the following from various sources.

>Not kings and lords, but nations!
>Not thrones and crowns but men!
>God save the people!
>>Ebenezer Elliott (1781-1849)

>...of the people, by the people, and for the people.
>>Abraham Lincoln

>The voice of the people is the voice of God.
>>Alcuin (735-804)
>>Letter to Charlemagne (800)

>The Lord showed me, so that I did see clearly, that he did not dwell in these temples which men had commanded and set up, but in people's hearts...his people were his temple, and he dwelt in them.
>>George Fox, Journal 16794 (See I Corinthians 3:16, 17)

>Let my people go.
>>Moses, Exodus 5:1

>The people are the most important element in a nation...
>>Mencino (372-289 B.C.)

>We are the people of his pasture and the sheep of his hand.
>>Psalm 95:7

Christian ministry centers in people. This premise has many implications. It is the practice of some to put the gospel in the center. They spend their efforts in getting the message over through preaching, teaching and other means. Others put the Bible, the traditions, and history and heritage of the faith into central position. Still others give their greatest emphasis to the church as an institution. All these are essential to the ministry. We cannot do without any of them. However, according to Jesus, they are secondary to persons; and are to be used as resources in serving human beings.

Jesus is our model for this principle. He used the scriptures, the religious institutions of his day and the heritage of Judaism, to serve the people.

Further, time and again he set aside, ignored, went against or beyond any of these if they interfered with filling human need. For example, one Sabbath he and his disciples were walking through a wheat field. They were hungry. They had had no food though it was mealtime. The law was that one should do no threshing on the Sabbath. Jesus ignored the law; he and his friends gathered the heads of wheat, threshed them by rubbing the heads between their hands, and began to eat the kernels. Their hunger took precedence over law and tradition.[4]

The reading of all the gospels, and the "golden text of the Bible" exemplify how human beings were put into the heart of God's intentional love.

---

[4] Matthew 12:1-8; 12:9-14; John 5:1-18; 8:1-11; 9:1-18; 10:1-16.

> For God so loved the world that he gave his only son that whoever believes in him should not perish but have eternal life.[5]

The focus of God's love is a WHO, not a WHAT.

To make people the main concern in our regard carries us much farther than we may realize at first. It means we have to include everyone. No one is shut out, regardless of how great or small they may seem to be by the standards of the world.

Redemption embraces all people, all kinds of people, people everywhere and anywhere: young and old; rich and poor; red and yellow, black and white; educated and uneducated; healthy and unhealthy; lovable and unlovable; the born and the unborn.

Moreover, following the model of Christ will get us deeply involved in all sorts of lives and lifestyles at close range. This entanglement can result in a rich mixture of opportunities which challenge, demand and bless, and at times frustrate and disturb. These are the risks we have to run, however, if we do ministry.

This openness and tender caring is the distinct opposite of a cheap professionalism which uses people for its own ends; such as manipulating them to build success symbols instead of serving them in the name and spirit of Jesus Christ.

Ministering to people requires as much knowledge and understanding of them as is possible. It asks that we read and study in the fields of psychology and sociology. This does not mean we have to become professionals; we can search for fundamental information in its simplest forms. There are many resources available for this purpose.

We also need information concerning the individuals and families we serve. It is essential for us to come to an understanding of the family as a system.

Further knowledge to inform our ministry is familiarity with the nature and characteristics of persons with various national, cultural and ethnic backgrounds.

Further still, it is important to remind ourselves that all people need and want very much the same things, such as an adequate income, a home, health, education, freedom, justice, acceptance, love, status, recognition, fairness and a religion that is real.

In addition to what has been said, it is incumbent that pastors know what is going on in the world. A notable theologian and author has said that the minister should read with the Bible in one hand and the daily newspaper in the other. People are the source of the very best and the very worst of news. We should know as much about them as possible.

A MINISTRY OF RECONCILIATION

> Reconciliation is the word in the NT to describe the changed relations between God and man which are the result of the death and resurrection of Jesus. To reconcile is the distinctive activity of God himself, and the world of men is the object of reconciliation...Reconciliation has the significance of a

---

[5] John 3:16.

new stage in personal relationships in which previous hostility of mind or estrangement has been put away in some decisive act.[6]

The gospel is the good news of God's seeking love in Jesus Christ. It is the good news of reconciliation. Jesus sought everywhere for lost sheep.[7]

God took the initiative in sending Jesus Christ to reconcile us. When Jesus came, he reached out to bring people into a relation with God and with each other. The Great Shepherd did not and does not wait for human beings to begin their search for salvation; on the contrary, God makes the prior move. At the point we are awakened to a need for God, and begin our search, it is certain God has already come to us and moved us toward a response, like the good shepherd looking for the lost sheep, and like the outreaching love of the father drawing the prodigal home.

> God acts to restore sinful persons to a covenant relationship, the nature of which is that of a family. It is established through God's initiative and the human response of faith.[8]

> He chose us in him before the foundation of the world, that we should be holy and blameless before him. He destined us in love to be his children through Jesus Christ, according to the purpose of his will.[9]

The fact of God seeking us out is either one of the biggest pieces of foolishness in the world, or it is one of the most incomprehensible wonders. It overwhelms the mind. It is beyond grasping. Think of it! The Creator and Redeemer seeking out the most forgotten and neglected human being! Coming even to you and me! This good news should be shouted from the housetop and embodied in every congregation that names the name of Christ. Indeed, it is for this that we have been commissioned. How can we be so calm and quiet about it?

> The church...is commissioned to witness to all persons who have not received Christ as Lord and Savior.[10]

> Go into all the world and preach the gospel...[11]

> How beautiful are the feet of those who preach good news![12]

How can we be moved to this mission with fervor? Have we not already been touched by contemplating the wondrous love of God? If we have caring hearts we

---

[6] *A Theological Word Book of the Bible*, Alan Richardson, Macmillan, page 185.

[7] Luke 15:1-10; Romans 5:1-12; II Corinthians 5:17-21; Ephesians 2; Colossians 1:19-22.

[8] *The Confession of Faith*, page 5, Section 3.02.

[9] Ephesians 1:4, 5; John 4:44.

[10] *The Confession of Faith*, page 15, Section 5.28.

[11] Mark 16:15.

[12] Romans 10:15.

will be disturbingly aroused when we think of all the alienation, estrangement, hostility, conflict, abuse and inhumanity in our world. The whole human race groans and travails for redemption.

A MINISTRY OF PREACHING AND TEACHING

Jesus came preaching and teaching.[13]

He proclaimed the good news of the kingdom of God. He declared God's sovereign rule, and called upon everyone to repent and believe. His was the affirming word that God is in control of all creation and will fulfil every promise made in the Scriptures. God's purpose will prevail. The kingdom of justice, truth and love will come. Although God's rule may be hidden at present, it will be vindicated in the future. Evil will be destroyed and God's righteousness will be supreme. This heartening affirmation calls for declaration in our shaky world today. What a faith to proclaim!

Further, he announced the good news that salvation is available to everyone. Whosoever will may be saved. All of us can be delivered:

> from darkness to light, from alienation to a share in divine citizenship, from guilt to pardon, from slavery to freedom, from fear of hostile powers to liberty and assurance.[14]

Every living soul can be redeemed, brought back into the original relation with God, delivered from whatever chain may imprison it. This offer and promise gives hope to all who are trapped in their addiction and enslavement. Think of the millions who need to hear!

Jesus also came teaching. They called him the master teacher. He gave rise to a teaching ministry in his church. The gospels contain large segments of his teaching. They indicate how much importance he gave to it and how much time he spent in doing it.[15]

Proclamation is the offer of salvation in Christ; teaching has to do with the ethical implications of the gospel as it is lived out every day. The 1883 *Confession of Faith* refers to ministers as "teaching elders." The 1984 *Confession* denotes "teacher" as one of the roles of the minister. We are to follow in the footsteps of the master teacher.

A MINISTRY OF FORGIVENESS

Jesus sought to restore broken relationships with God through forgiveness. He preached and taught the love, mercy and grace of God, who cares for all persons and calls them into covenant relationship. Jesus exemplified the qualities of love and mercy, and was seldom judgmental except toward the unrepentant leaders of the religious establishment.[16]

---

[13] Mark 1:14, 15; Matthew 4:23; 5:1, 2.

[14] *A Theological Word Book*, Alan Richardson, Macmillan, page 220.

[15] Examples: Matthew 5:6, 7; Luke 6:17-49; Matthew 13, Mark 4, Luke 15, 16; John 6; 8:12-20; 10:1-21; 14, 15.

[16] Examples of Jesus' loving spirit: Luke 7:36-50; Luke 19:1-10; John 4:1-26; 8:1-11.

His message was that love forgives, heals and reconciles. He preached both love and judgment; not just one or the other. He said sin is wrong, but God loves and forgives; God's offer of forgiveness is accepted through faith.[17]

The ministry of forgiveness is timely and essential. We all sin and need forgiveness. Many are burdened by guilt and feel helpless and condemned. Their condition cries out for the grace and love of God who can make them whole.

For this message to become effective, the church must embody the ministry of forgiveness in its whole life, not merely in its words. It is called to live with outreach and openness, acceptance and love; not judgment and rejection. It is to become a warm and loving family through which the gospel is communicated.

Paul concluded the twelfth chapter of I Corinthians, which was about life in the body of Christ, by saying, "I will show you a still more excellent way." The more excellent way was the way of love, described in First Corinthians 13. A young man who had lived a bad life once said to a minister, "I just need someone to love me." In this broken world there are multitudes who need that. God intends for the church to do it.

A SERVANT MINISTRY

"The servant is bent to the shape of another's need." Jesus' ministry was a servant ministry. He was bent to the shape of humanity's need. The church has interpreted his ministry in terms of the servant figure.[18] Jesus made it clear to his disciples that his ministry and theirs were interrelated; and that it was to be a servant ministry.[19] The implications of this fact are far-reaching.

Jesus was a *suffering* servant. His life came to a climax on the cross. There is no ministry without some kind of suffering, either inwardly or outwardly. Henri Nouwen corroborates that beautifully in one of his books.[20] This concept belies the idea many have that ministry is a career and that ministers should seek all the benefits of other professions. Ministers should be paid a fair remuneration and given other benefits. It is a matter of emphasis. Will they be more aware of benefits than doing their ministry? For some it seems so. It is incumbent upon congregations to give full consideration to the needs of ministers and their families. It is incumbent upon ministers to keep a balance in their expectations and requests. One's image affects one's ministry. Let it be one of a servant, not a hireling. This is not meant to support sessions who negotiate salaries to the lowest possible amount.

The cross vindicated Jesus and his ministry; crossbearing makes ours valid and effective. Whatever suffering ministers may experience, however, let it be done quietly and unobtrusively.

> He was oppressed, and he was afflicted, yet he opened not his mouth, and like a lamb that is led to the slaughter, and like a sheep that before its shearers is dumb, so he opened not his mouth.[21]

---

[17] Romans 3:9-16; 5:1-11; 8:1-17.

[18] See Isaiah 42:1-4; 49:1-6; 52:13—53:12; 61:1-3.

[19] Read Matthew 20:24-28; Luke 22:24-27; John 13:1-16; Philippians 2:5-11.

[20] *The Wounded Healer*, Henri Nouwen, Doubleday, 1972.

[21] Isaiah 53:7.

Suffering which is overdramatized, or vocalized, loses its effectiveness.

If we must talk about suffering, let it be to a counselor. Some find this to be necessary. Many ministers experience burn-out from the stress they are under. What is said above is not to ignore this fact or to be unsympathetic about it; but rather is meant to be a word of caution about talking to everyone about our pains. Remember there are others who hurt also. Pain borne gracefully opens doors to empathetic and healing relationships.

What we are saying may seem to have been written only for the clergy. However, the basic principles apply to laypersons as well. The parable of the Good Samaritan supports the idea that helping persons often requires us to go out of our way. This may entail forbearance, patience, anxiety and even pain. Service is seldom a pleasant do-gooders game.

A MINISTRY OF HEALING, COMFORT AND ENCOURAGEMENT

Human need drained Jesus' life-giving force as he healed the sick, made the blind to see and the deaf to hear. He was vulnerable to all who were hurting. He drew needy people to him, sending none of them away. His heart went out to them. This was the way he was.

Jesus is our model. Although we cannot heal as he did, our caring response to people who suffer has a healing influence beyond measure. There are those who publicize, televise and over-dramatize their healing powers. Many of them are charlatans. Care is cautioned in this matter of healing. Yet, all of us, if we truly care, can be healers in the name and spirit of Jesus Christ. Anyone who listens with a hearing and empathetic ear to those who are pouring out their souls in anguish is a healer.

Jesus also gave *comfort* to people. *Comfort* means *to strengthen*. It also suggests empathy, which is feeling *with*, rather than feeling sorry *for*. When Jesus spoke to a person, or listened, or touched, he did it in love. Because he identified with others, great comfort and peace of mind resulted. Perhaps some of the best ministry we may do is in face to face contact relieving people in their life struggle.

Jesus also was an *encourager*. He did not put people down. They always felt more positive about themselves after being with him. He gave them hope. He made them feel they were somebody. This, too, is a part of our work. How do we make people feel about themselves?

A DISTURBING MINISTRY

This may appear to be a contradiction to what has been said about comfort. An often repeated saying is that "Jesus came to comfort the disturbed and to disturb the comfortable." Jesus did disturb the comfortable in many ways. He spoke some words about this which are often hard to understand. For instance, he said he had come not to bring peace but a sword.[22] He may have viewed his ministry as a means of bringing conflict so people would have to make choices they otherwise might not have made.

Jesus disturbed the people of Nazareth at the outset of his ministry. He read from Isaiah 61:1-4 and claimed that in him those words were fulfilled. This was to

---

[22] Matthew 10:34-39.

be the nature of his ministry. The people became so angry that they tried to destroy him.[23]

After the first phase of his work Jesus came into conflict with the powerful group of religious leaders who controlled the temple. His teachings, his popularity among the common people, his indifference to, and the breaking of, many of their traditions disturbed them deeply. The conflict became exceedingly hot when he ran the moneychangers out of the temple.[24]

The sixth chapter of John records an event in which many of Jesus' disciples became greatly disturbed and left him. He seemed to demand more than they were willing to give.[25]

Jesus disturbed the people of Gadara when he healed a demoniac in that region. They were so upset, because of fear or because he had destroyed a herd of pigs, that they wanted him to get out of their country.[26]

What is implied here for our ministry?

A WHOLE MINISTRY

The ministry is *a whole ministry.*[27] It is interrelated in all its aspects. Everything Jesus did was integrated into a whole. So must ours be. We cannot let one person be the preacher, another a pastoral visitor, another a director of Christian education, still another the business manager, with each working separately as if their particular work is the ministry of greatest importance. It has to be done in mutual relationships. All parts must participate together.

Can preaching be done effectively apart from visitation, or teaching, or administering, or vice versa? Neither can we separate our preaching from our visiting, our teaching from our preaching, our administering from our caring. Nor can the laity carry on one kind of ministry and the pastor another. Both are to be involved in the whole ministry as one.

A MINISTRY BY THE ENTIRE CHURCH

Let us emphasize again the place of the laity in Christian ministry.

Baptism and confirmation are the primary ordination to the ministry of Jesus Christ to which all else is secondary; in short, according to the scripture, one cannot be a Christian without receiving the Spirit of God, which is always empowerment for a ministry.[28]

This concept cuts across one often found in our churches, which is, that members are receivers, not givers; they are to be served by their minister-servants; they are to be saved, assured of heaven, comforted and to be made to enjoy their religion. In many congregations the laity on the whole are not asked to serve and

---

[23] Luke 4:16-30.

[24] Matthew 21:12-17.

[25] John 6:66-69.

[26] Luke 8:26-39.

[27] Ephesians 4:1-7.

[28] *The Rebirth of Ministry*, James D. Smart, Westminster, page 12. *Note:* I am indebted to Dr. Smart for some of the basic concepts of ministry.

are given no training to do so. Yet, note how many lay persons are actually serving, whether or not they have formal or informal training.

The Scriptures, the doctrine, and the heritage of our Protestant faith, teach that every Christian is a minister.[29]

> Probably the doctrine most misunderstood by both Roman Catholics and Protestants, and most neglected by Protestants, is the priesthood of all believers. It affirms that every [person] is God's minister, that each person is [his or her] own priest, but with a social responsibility; therefore, each person is...priest [to others]... The fuller and truer meaning is that every [person] is [his or her] own priest only insofar as [he or she] belongs to the 'mutual ministry of all believers.' In the fellowship of believers [the Christian] is united 'in the communion of the forgiven and forgiving.'[30]

According to this principle the clergy and laity stand on equal ground. Christian ministry is to be done by the entire church. Every member is to serve the church and to serve through the church.

The antithesis of this idea is often expressed in words similar to the following, based on the notion that the main purpose of the church is to serve its members: "This church is not meeting my needs. I must find one that does." We must do our best to replace this attitude.

SUMMARY

In reviewing the ideas so far in this chapter, we find that Christian ministry is the ministry of Jesus Christ; it centers in people; it is a ministry of reconciliation; preaching and teaching; forgiveness; a servant ministry; a ministry of healing, comfort and encouragement; a disturbing ministry; a whole ministry; and a ministry done by the entire church.

These are guidelines without which we are lost and lack understanding of our mission.

THE ROLES AND RESPONSIBILITIES OF THE MINISTER

We turn now to the *practice* of ministry. Our understanding of its nature must be translated into special functions and responsibilities in order to facilitate its fulfillment. It is important to see our work in terms of its various parts and particulars in order to take hold of it.

The scope of our responsibilities is wide and inclusive. Ministers are generalists; not specialists. They do many things rather than centering on only one. Their calling demands a variety of talents and skills for their many functions. There is no end to their search for knowledge of how to practice their vocation. This means they need continuing education. This is especially true of the pastors of congregations.

---

[29] Read I Peter 2:5, 9.

[30] *I Am A Protestant*, Ray Freeman Jenney, Bobbie Merrill, page 86.

A SCRIPTURAL LIST OF MINISTRIES

There are at least six (6) listings of offices, gifts, titles and functions of Ministry in the New Testament. Roles for the ministry are derived from this biblical foundation.[31] There are repetitions in these lists. If you read through them you will find at least ten (10) categories. They are:

- Prophets or Prophecy
- Apostles
- Serving, such as healing, miracles, helpers
- Teaching, knowledge, teachers, distinguishing between spirits, interpretation, interpreters
- Pastors
- Administrators
- Evangelists
- Contributors
- Exhortations
- Tongues

MINISTERS OF THE WORD AND SACRAMENT

Our *Confession of Faith* in Sections 2.61-2.64 of the Constitution, names eight (8) functions of the ministry.[32] It also treats some of the ideas already mentioned here.

CONSIDER THESE ROLES FOR THE MINISTER

Congregations have role expectations for the minister. Ministers have certain role expectations for themselves. It is important to arrive at a mutual understanding between the congregation and the minister concerning these roles. A generally acceptable set of roles for the minister, based upon Scripture, *The Confession of Faith*, observation, history and tradition is given below. Most ministers perform these roles at one time or another. It is essential to keep them in balance. They are given here as a set of authentic roles for your ministry.

Preacher: One who proclaims the gospel of Christ. Preaching is central in the functions of our ministry. We think of its being done primarily to a congregation. It may also be done to small groups, to individuals, to "accidental audiences," in church, on the streets, in homes, and also during pastoral visits. It can be done briefly or at length.

Prophet: One who proclaims the will of God for *all* of life. The prophet speaks to social ills and calls upon people and nations to obey the word of God, warning them of the results of their failure. This role should be performed with care and thoughtfulness; and with the knowledge that it arouses resistance. It should be done in the pastoral context.

Pastor: One who is a shepherd, a care giver, who leads and feeds the flock with spiritual food. The pastor is approachable, and is available to the people for problem-solving, visiting and counseling, making the first move in offering

---

[31] Refer to Romans 12:6-8; I Corinthians 12:8-10; I Corinthians 12:28; Acts 13:1; I Peter 4:11; Ephesians 4:7, 11, 12.

[32] *The Confession of Faith*, pages 30, 31.

pastoral services. Warmth, compassion and firmness mark the true pastor.

Priest: One who is the mediator, interceding between God and the people. The priest leads the people in worship, in prayer, in celebrating the sacraments, and in preserving the Christian heritage. The priest strives to make ritual the channel for God's grace by doing it well.

Teacher: One who instructs believers in the scriptures and other Christian literature with emphasis upon Christian growth and becoming equipped for Christian ministry.

Educator: One who has a grasp of educational principles and leads in planning and administering the educational work of the congregation. As teacher-educator the minister should consider this to be one of his or her major responsibilities which should not be delegated to anyone unequipped in this area. The minister-educator works with the session and a responsible task force or committee in this concern.

Administrator: One who takes the lead in managing the whole work of the church, providing guidance to the end that the life and work of the church run smoothly and effectively. An administrator may be thought of as a manager. Management is shared with the session.

Organizer: One who helps set goals, develops concepts and program activities for the congregation, working with the session and committees.

Leader: One who initiates, takes the lead, but who does not "run things" autocratically. A good leader elicits leadership from others and delegates duties and authority. Most churches expect the minister to take the lead. Leadership is shared with the session.

Elder or presbyter: One who shares in the leadership and government of the church. In the Cumberland Presbyterian Church, with its connectional type of government, the minister is obligated to share responsibility in the congregation, the presbytery, the synod and the general assembly.

These roles and responsibilities should be kept in balance in the practice of ministry.

FOR FURTHER CONSIDERATION

- How much information do you have about the people whom you serve?
- How much knowledge do you have of the characteristics of the various stages of human growth? Children, Youth, Adults, Middle Adults, Older Adults?
- How much have you read about the family as a system?
- Do you keep up with the events of the day which affect the people of your church?
- How would you define reconciliation?
- If you are, or plan to become, a member of the clergy, do you think of yourself as a teaching elder as well as a preacher? How much study have you done in the field of Christian education?
- What can you do to enable a congregation to become a fellowship of forgivers?
- What kinds of suffering do you think you are doing as a minister?
- Can you name the ten roles of the minister? Would you add others? If so, what? These roles seem to apply exclusively to the ordained clergy. What do they say to you as a lay person?

BOOKS FOR FURTHER READING

The First Parish, J. Keith Cook, Westminster, 1983, 154 pages
Putting It Together in the Parish, James D. Glasse, Abingdon, 1972, 159 pages
Creative Ministry, Henry J. M. Nouwen, Double Day & Company, 1971, 119 pages

SOMETHING TO REFLECT UPON

As you look at the many responsibilities of the Christian minister, you may rightly wonder how you do it all. It is such a demanding task. The truth is, no one can do it perfectly. No one can possibly do all that is expected. One has to do the very best possible, and lean heavily upon the Holy Spirit. Spend some time thinking about this.

CHAPTER 2

The Call to Ministry

Let's begin where you are. You believe you have been called to the ministry of Word and Sacrament. Or as a lay person you may feel called to serve as an unordained Christian. Below is a picture of "Go Preach" by Eugene Burnand, 1850-1921. It is an illustration of the scripture, "Go into all the world and preach the

EUGENE BURNAND, SWISS, 1850-1921. PHOTO: RUDOLF LESCH FINE ARTS.

gospel to every creature." Mark 16:15. It was drawn after 1908. Take a good look at it and read the meditation that follows.

> Here is the Great Commission reduced to simplest terms: a personal appeal for loyalty and service, from a great teacher to his pupil. It is not the historic Jesus of Nazareth calling Peter or John; it is the eternal Christ appealing to young people [and others]—in every land, through all the centuries. Burnand names the picture "Go Preach," but he might as well have named it Go Teach or Go Sell or Go Paint or Plow or Sing. He has really dramatized the eternal

call of God to the human heart, the eternal urge by which God drives men [and women] toward higher things. Christ is here pointing out a way of life, summoning youth to follow an ideal, to accept a companionship, to assume a task.

How does one know that?

First observe the face and eyes of Christ. They bear the stamp of the dreamer, the idealist. The eyes are raised a little above the level of earth and they are not converged upon an object. They are seeing things in the large rather than in detail; the mind behind them is occupied with principles and grand objectives; and the hand, that a lesser artist would have made to point to something specific, is merely suggesting something vague, over the horizon, up in the heavens.

Next look at the young man's face. The brow is contracted, the eyes are sharply focused and converged upon a distant object. The disciple is earnestly trying to make out a specific goal, a task in time and place to which he may address himself; something to work out, accomplish. There is no vagueness in his mind about this call; there is nothing ethereal in it. He is about to tackle a 'job.'

The difference in the two faces is intentional. Burnand has interpreted correctly the historic and perpetual relationship between Christ and his disciples. Christ has a vision of a world redeemed, of the kingdom of God, [the kinship of all human beings], human nature transformed by love from selfishness and individualism to organization and co-operation. That is a grand and compelling ideal that is indeed over the horizon and partly in the clouds, but it grips men [and women] powerfully, especially young men and women, and sets them on fire for service. But the ideal must be interpreted in practical terms and made operative in concrete ways. The general must be embodied in the particular.

Down through the ages young enthusiasts have picked out their specific jobs, their own limited and human objectives. Paul sees his task to be founding churches, Dorcas making coats for the poor at Joppa, Athanasius working out a trinitarian formula for the creed. Ambrose trains choirs to enrich the liturgy at Milan. Charlemagne founds a hospital for pilgrims in Jerusalem. Saint Francis washes the wounds of lepers and weds Lady Poverty. Bernard preaches a crusade. Luther nails his world-shaking challenge on the church at Wittenberg. Cromwell leads his Ironsides against tyranny. Howard reforms the prison system of England. Wilberforce frees slaves. George Williams founds the Y.M.C.A. Arnold Toynbee devises a social settlement. Parkhurst fights Tammany. Theodore Roosevelt 'busts trusts.' Jane Addams brings hope to youth on the city streets. Millions down through the ages have caught the vision of God's kingdom over the horizon, in the sky, and have followed the Gleam each in his own way to a finite and definite end; and always under the inspiration of the Great Captain. [Think of others in more recent years.]

What a wonderful partnership it is! The challenge and the response, the infinite and the finite, the far-off ideal and the task near at hand.

Do you notice that the left arm of Christ is around the young man's shoulder, that Christ's head bends slightly toward the other's, and that the great cloak covers both persons? That is the artist's way of saying: 'Lo, I am with you always'; 'Having loved his own, he loved them until the end'; 'What shall separate us from the love of Christ?' 'I in them and thou in me'; 'I can do all things in him that strengthens me.'

Stamp this picture on your memory. It will steady you, help you think straight, and give you courage.[1]

GOD CALLS EVERYONE

The call to the ministry of Word and Sacrament needs to be discussed in view of a wide perspective similar to the interpretation above; that is, in the light of our assumption that God calls everyone. It is the Cumberland Presbyterian belief that God calls all persons into a covenant relationship. It is a call to salvation and an offer of a redemptive relationship with God, a call to a life dedicated to following Jesus Christ.

It is he who brought us salvation and called us to a dedicated life, not for any merit of ours but of his own purpose and his own grace.[2]

God acted redemptively in Jesus Christ because of the sins of the world and continues with the same intent in the Holy Spirit to call every person to repentance and faith.[3]

Once we have entered into this relationship with God through Jesus Christ, we can expect that there may be other calls to various kinds of service; or to say the least, we have made ourselves open to them.

GOD CALLS EVERYONE TO SERVICE

Further, it is the biblical understanding that we are not only called to salvation, but to service. Baptism may be thought of as a kind of ordination to that end. Any work we do can be considered as a vocation of God through which we can minister. It is true that many do not put this meaning into their work. Some would find it difficult to do so because of the nature of their occupation. Still, there are many who do. A friend once said to the son of a farmer who was plowing his cotton nearby, "Every time that cultivator wheel turns over, it is a prayer from your father's heart." Although it is difficult to put this ideal into practice in our thing-centered world, it is essential for Christians to make serious efforts to work it out in their lives, making their occupations true callings.

Both the Old and New Testaments record instances of people being called to vocation: Moses to lead the people of God to the Promised Land, Samuel hearing the call of God as a child, Aaron called to the priesthood, David called to be a king, Jeremiah understanding that he had been appointed prophet even from his mother's womb, Jesus calling disciples to follow.

Yes. As astounding as it may seem in this secular world, God does call everyone to salvation and service.

---

[1] From *Pictures in the Upper Room*, Interpretations by Albert Edward Bailey, copyright © 1940 by The Upper Room, 1908 Grand Avenue, P.O. Box 189, Nashville, TN 37202. Used by permission of the publisher.

[2] II Timothy 1:9 NEB.

[3] *Confession of Faith*, Cumberland Presbyterian Church, Section 4.01, page 7.

GOD CALLS LAY PERSONS TO SERVE IN THE CHURCH

We have been thinking about those who are called to make their work a vocation of God, and those who have been assigned specific tasks. We should not omit some others. What about the great numbers of persons who serve in the congregations and the church at large as lay people throughout the whole world? Most of them make their living by some kind of secular work. Because of their abilities and training they either volunteer, or are recruited, for service in the congregation. They serve as elders, deacons, task force members, board members, teachers, administrators, officers in CPW and similar organizations, leaders of youth and other age groups, presbyters, and in many other ways.

All of these persons are in the ministry also. Can they not believe that they have been called to service? God calls through abilities, talents, opportunities, needs, situations and through the official channels of the church. All these are legitimate servants of the Lord and are ministers in their own rights and responsibilities. Some of them are ordained and others are set apart in special services of dedication for their duties. These are numbered among the saints mentioned in Ephesians 4:12, who have been equipped for ministry.

GOD CALLS SOME TO BE MINISTERS OF WORD AND SACRAMENT

Still further, there are those who receive a call to be ministers of the Word and Sacrament. They are summoned to serve in and through the church, and beyond, under proper authority.

Biblically, the church is both the agent and the authenticating voice of the call. The church has always been the one to legitimize the call. There is no effective calling, nor authoritative ordination, apart from the church.

When Jesus was no longer present in body, the apostles became the body to call and authorize. Remember the eleven, under God's guidance, acting to make Matthias an apostle?[4] Remember also Paul's conversion. As powerful and convincing as it was, God used those in the church to authenticate the commission Paul had received. He was sent to Ananias of Damascus who helped Paul understand what had happened to him.[5] Beware of any tendency in yourself, or any act on the part of others, to assume authority independently of the church!

THE MYSTERY OF THE CALL

Let us think for a moment of the mystery of God's summons to us. The fact that we are elected to a relationship with God, and for the ministry, is a source of awe, wonder and often disbelief. It is more than we can comprehend; and the wonder of it is overwhelming. *Me?* Why would God call *me?* Why would the God of the universe be aware of me and want me to be a minister? Of course, we have been taught that God cares for each of us and wants us to serve; when it comes to our own personal experience, it is almost more than we can accept. Sometimes our own friends and family members question it; perhaps more out of amazement than doubt.

---

[4] Acts 1:26.

[5] Acts 22:14, 15

Each of us experiences the mandate in our own particular way. Perhaps all of us, however, find some common factors in it. Have we not all experienced something like the following: There is an urgent sense that God is calling us. It never lets up. It is a drawing, a wooing, a tugging, coming strongly at times, weaker at others, but never abating altogether. There is often, but not always, resistance and reluctance and excuse, and sometimes, refusal. Finally, it becomes a conviction that we are chosen, called and commissioned by God to the ministry of Word and Sacrament, that we are "called to preach" and "Woe is me if I preach not the gospel."

HOW THE CALL MAY COME

The call may come directly to a person, and/or through various means. Can you identify with any of the following?

The call may come through:

1. *The life and fellowship of the church and the influence of the gospel in our lives.* In other words, it arises out of our own Christian experience which kindles an interest and a desire to do more.

2. *The suggestions of well meaning people.* They may ask at some time and place, "Have you ever considered the ministry?" Thus the idea is dropped into our minds. They may have observed something about us which indicated that we had the ability to become a minister.

3. *The spiritual atmosphere* of the congregation, a conference, a church camp, or some other group may have moved us and brought the call into focus.

4. *God may speak to us through a time of worship* and/or a sermon in which the idea was born in our minds or the impression made upon us.

5. *The influence of ministers.* We may see something in them which appeals to us and makes us want to be like them. They become good models. They may be pastors or parents whose children may follow in their footsteps.

6. *A direct confrontation* by some person: "Have you ever considered the ministry? Can you say you have not been called?" In the early years of our denomination such recruitment was done more than it is today.

7. *A recognition on our part* of having some ability for the ministry.

8. *A challenge of need and opportunity.* Upon hearing about or observing the need for ministers, we may be challenged to consider it.

9. Or, through other means, such as *a growing conviction* over a period of time that the ministry is God's will for us. Interviews with a number of people in recent years indicate that this is the kind of experience many have had.

THE CUMBERLAND PRESBYTERIAN CHURCH AND A GOD-CALLED MINISTRY

In the early days of our denomination it was believed that if persons were called to the ministry they were able in the sense that they had the equipment. There seemed to be little questioning of one's fitness for the occupation. This did not mean they needed no education, for the church set standards for ordination and provided educational opportunities.

This practice has continued throughout the years. If someone says he or she is called to the ministry, seldom are any questions asked. We are gradually learning that it would be a service to the church if some questioning were done in order to protect the church from those not fit emotionally or otherwise for the task, and to keep persons from making harmful mistakes about their life work. Probably all of us know cases in which persons have proved to be unfit for the work and have had to drop out. This has been very painful for them and others and has not helped the church. In some cases harm has been done. This gives cause for all of us to make sure of God's will for our lives, especially if we are considering the gospel ministry.

Officially, the church does not accept the fact that if a person is called he or she is ready for ministry. The church has set standards for ordination. In the process of being educated for the ministry one has the chance to become sure of his or her calling and be fully confirmed, or to make a change. It has been suggested by some that psychological and aptitude tests be given to aid one in deciding.

Regardless, we believe the call is essential. It does many things for us, among which are three that are very important: (1) it authorizes us; (2) it motivates us; (3) it sustains us, holds us to the task.

The Cumberland Presbyterian Church has accepted and stated in its official documents what it believes about a God-called ministry. It used the *Westminster Confession*, with some modifications, at its outset. This *Confession* states:

> It is the duty of the presbytery, for their satisfaction with regard to the real piety of such candidates, to examine them respecting their experimental acquaintance with religion, and the motives which influence them to desire the sacred office.[6]

Note: No specific reference is made to a call.

The 1814 *Confession of Faith* of the Cumberland Presbyterian Church, a revision of the *Westminster Confession*, states:

> It is the duty of the presbytery, for their satisfaction with regard to the real piety of such candidates, to examine them respecting their experimental acquaintance with religion, and the motives which influence them to desire the sacred office, and their internal call to this important work.[7]

Note: Our church forebears added the last sentence.

The 1883 *Confession of Faith* of the Cumberland Presbyterian Church makes the same statement as the one above.[8]

The 1984 *Confession of Faith* of the Cumberland Presbyterian Church states:

> The committee on the ministry shall examine candidates respecting personal religious experience, motives leading to the seeking of the office of the ministry and the internal call to it, *and plans for education.*[9]

---

[6] *Westminster Confession of Faith,* 1729, page 375.

[7] 1814 *Confession of Faith,* page 93.

[8] 1883 *Confession of Faith,* page 111.

[9] 1984 *Confession of Faith,* page 45.

Note: The revisers added the last phrase. The same is said about the licentiate but a little more is added.

Mahlon's Letters, bound in book form, were addressed to his nephew and published in 1867. Here is one quote about the call.

> As Presbyterians, we believe in a call to the ministry. That is, God selects from among men, and impresses with a sense of duty those whom he desires as his ambassadors to a world of sinners. And these impressions are of such character that he who receives them need not remain in doubt as to their import.[10]

Note: Cumberland Presbyterians did not write a great deal about the call to the ministry. It seems to have been one of those beliefs that lived by its own strength, and was communicated from one generation to another.

For more about the call to the ministry you may read *A People Called Cumberland Presbyterian*, Frontier Press, 1972, Barrus, Baughn, Campbell, pages 189-192.

SOME QUESTIONS FOR FURTHER THOUGHT

Why have you entered the ministry? The Motives?

Do you feel you were called into it?

Can you describe briefly the call as it has come to you? Put it into five sentences. Write it down before you share it.

In one sentence, how would you explain to your children or teenagers why you are entering the ministry? (This for those who enter the ministry later)

How would you explain to your committee on the ministry or presbytery why you are entering the ministry?

ORDINATION: COMMITTEES ON THE MINISTRY, AND CANDIDATES

We are considering the meaning of ordination in the same chapter with the call to ministry. They are interrelated. Ordination may be seen as the confirmation of the call.

Candidates for the ministry often get in a hurry to be ordained. There are many reasons for this. Some have entered the ministry late and they feel time is running out on them. Some feel because they have been called, they want to get to work as soon as possible. They are full of zeal and impatience. If they are already serving churches, they feel they are handicapped by not being able to receive members, moderate the session, perform weddings and celebrate the sacraments. Often it is difficult to secure the aid of an ordained minister for some of these purposes. Sometimes congregations and sessions put pressure on the candidates to get ordained. Occasionally they may approach the committee on the ministry for this purpose.

There have been occasions when committees on the ministry have been slow in moving candidates toward ordination. This can produce tension and make it difficult to have the most satisfying and creative relations between candidates and the committees.

---

[10] *Mahlon's Letters*, 1867, page 27, 28.

On the other hand, the attitudes of candidates can contribute to good or bad relations. It would benefit the candidates to remember that they are on the receiving end of the process and cannot afford even to appear to be pushing. They have placed themselves under the authority of the church. Their position calls for attitudes of humility, patience and acceptance. It is hoped that committees on the ministry will be sensitive to the hopes, aspirations and eagerness of the candidates; and that they will become aware of any problems candidates may be facing. The relationship calls for committees on the ministry to spend adequate time with candidates, counseling and instructing them, and even more important, encouraging them.

To be fair, this matter of progress toward ordination is a mutual responsibility between the candidates and the committees. It is urgent that both parties understand this and act accordingly. Committee members are usually busy persons and must adjust full schedules for their time with candidates. Candidates are often young and uninformed and have to deal with the adjustment usually demanded when one sets one's face toward such a great task. They need a lot of attention and care. If one enters the ministry later, there is a new set of problems which call for serious consideration. These factors indicate a dire need for mutual understanding.

Before candidates are ordained they need not only to meet educational requirements and acquire emotional and spiritual growth, they also need to come to understand clearly the meaning of ordination. Otherwise, they will be ill equipped for their work. Therefore, the next section will deal briefly and simply with these matters, introducing certain basic concepts with the hope that the subject may be more deeply considered as time goes by.

ORDINATION: SCRIPTURAL BACKGROUND AND MEANING[11]

The church has the right to declare the terms of admission into its communion, qualifications of its ministers, officers and member, and standards for ordination.

> Every Christian Church, or union, or association of particular Churches, has the right to declare the terms of admission into its communion, and the qualifications of its ministers, officers, and members, as well as the whole system of its internal government.[12]

We are a connectional church and higher judicatories usually set standards for the education and ordination of ministers which presbyteries usually accept. The power of ordination, however, is placed in the presbytery.

Laying on of hands is an ancient ritual, used in Bible times for a number of purposes. One in particular has to do with ordination. The word *ordain* means *to order aright*. Moses ordained Joshua as his successor.

---

[11] See *Interpreter's Bible Dictionary*, E-J, pages 521, 522.

[12] *Confession of Faith*, Cumberland Presbyterian Church, page vii, Section 7.

> The ordination of Joshua was an outward sign of recognition of Joshua's spiritual qualifications, and gave him authority to execute the office of leadership in the congregation of the people of God.[13]

Later the ceremony of laying on of hands was adopted for ordaining rabbis, which may well have been the source of Christian ordination.

In the New Testament ordination has the same sense and meaning. The seven were ordained by the twelve by prayers and laying on of hands.[14] Acts 13:3 records the laying on the hands by the prophets and teachers of Antioch to set apart Paul and Barnabas for their mission.

Paul writes about the gifts Timothy received at ordination. Ordination is more than an outward act, or rite; there is a dynamic in it.[15] God acts in ordination, setting apart certain persons for a special ministry, bestowing them with authority and power for their mission. God does not act autocratically. The candidate must be in a receptive mood. Thus, ordination is not to be conceived of as a matter of *status* to be sought for selfish or practical reasons; but it is an act by which one is consecrated to service, not merely a means for human recognition.

Note that in the scripture a person or a group with authority, did the laying on of hands. Further, according to the Bible, ordination is not done independently of the church. The church takes the responsibility of selecting, and preparing persons which it believes have the possibilities of ministry. It also assumes the right to set standards, and the responsibility of providing education.

One may ask where the church gets this authority. It comes from God who called the church into being and instituted the rite of ordination. God not only works through the individual to call that person, but God also works through the church to approve the call. Those who are ordained are under the authority of God through the church. They are answerable to someone beside themselves. It is important to believe this and to practice it; however, there are still some who act independently of the presbytery to which they belong. They reflect their biblical ignorance or stubbornness in so doing and deny the true nature of the church. According to our system of doctrine and government, the individual is not a law unto himself or herself, nor adequate alone. We are subject to one another. The individual needs the wisdom, guidance, instruction, support and encouragement of others.

With reference to Paul again, when he was converted, God appointed Ananias, a prophet of the church, to guide him, interpret the meaning of the call, and to teach him. Then, he worked under the call and approval of the church before he was sent out as a missionary with Barnabas. Later upon occasions when Paul was challenged and asked about his authority, he told the whole story of his conversion and how the church had guided him.

MORE SPECIFICALLY, WHAT DOES ORDINATION ACCOMPLISH?

How will candidates be different and do differently after ordination? What does ordination do for—or to—us? That is asking what God does through ordination.

---

[13] *Interpreter's Bible Dictionary*, E-J, pages 521. Numbers 8:19; 27:18-23; Deut. 34:9.

[14] Acts 6:6.

[15] I Timothy 4:14; II Timothy 1:6, 7.

Ordination confirms your call to the ministry.

You have been called, chosen of God. God did the choosing. You did the responding. Ordination confirms your call. The church is saying that it believes your call is authentic.

Ordination brings you into the long line of apostolic succession.

You are being made a part of that illustrious (and at times not so illustrious) multitude of God's servants whom God called and commissioned to the ministry of Jesus Christ. You are made a part of the apostolic succession. Think of it! This is quite a host of renowned and distinguished persons who have served through the centuries. The recognition of this honored relationship is both the source of elation and humility.

In spite of all the mistakes we Reformed Protestants are accused of making, or might have in fact, made, we declare here and now that when the Cumberland Presbyterian Church ordains persons they are authentic servants of God.

These facts alone give us pause to consider the multi-dimensional nature of ordination and not to seek or take it lightly.

Ordination sets you apart to the ministry of Jesus Christ.

You are consecrated to the ministry of Jesus Christ—who bent his life to the shape of others' needs; who washed the disciples feet; who "for the joy that was set before him, endured the cross, despising the shame…"

You are consecrated to the ministry of Jesus Christ—not to a ministry you have conceived, nor the ministry of a human institution, nor a service club program—but the ministry of Jesus Christ which has been committed by him to the church.

You are dedicated to the ministry of Jesus Christ—not to some current fad dreamed up by some self-appointed showman, nor to some segment of the gospel you might feel has been neglected and you have been called to initiate it, not to some original, unique Gospel originated by you which you feel the world has been waiting breathlessly for; but the ministry of Jesus Christ.

You are sanctified to the suffering ministry of Jesus Christ, not to a ministry of success, status, exploitation, ecclesiastical power, popularity, magic, easy conscience or instant gratification.

You are set apart to the *whole* ministry of Jesus Christ, which is a ministry of reconciliation, proclamation, forgiveness, suffering service centered in people.

Ordination communicates authority (better translated responsibility) to you.

When Moses, near the close of his life, laid his hands on Joshua to commission him to be the leader of Israel, God said to him, "You shall invest him with some of your authority…" Numbers 27:20.

What kind of authority are you receiving?

The authority of the call. If the people perceive you have indeed been called, they will accept your authority.

The authority of experience. That is, your "experimental acquaintance with religion," your relation with God. Jesus spoke with authority. This means the people felt he knew what he was talking about firsthand. When you preach the gospel you can do it with authority if you yourself have experienced it fully.

Sacramental authority. You now have the privilege and sacred responsibility to celebrate the sacraments of baptism and the Lord's Supper.

Civic authority. You can now join people together in holy matrimony. In view of the tentative nature of many marriages today, this authority is to be treated sacredly with the intention of your doing all you can to make the marriage relationship an enduring one for those whom you bless in God's name.

Ministerial authority. You can now be pastor of a church, the spiritual overseer and shepherd of the flock.

Ecclesiastical authority. You can moderate the session, lead and administer the church program, exercise your rights as presbyter, be a commissioner to general Assembly, serve on church boards and represent your church in ecumenical relationships.

Accept authority with caution and exercise it in the same way. Much of it has to be earned in the old fashioned way, by working and waiting for it with patience and tact. The truth is, you have only as much authority as the people will invest in you.

Ordination Communicates Power (a Spirit) to You.

God is active in the laying on of hands and the worship of which it is a part. Through this ceremony God communicates spiritual power to you. (God does this at many other times, places and ways also.)

Consider what Paul said to Timothy about his ordination. "Hence I remind you to rekindle the gift of God that is within you through the laying on of my hands; for God did not give us a spirit of timidity, but a spirit of power and love and self-control.[16]

The power is the power of relationships, the power that comes from our relation with God. Without it we are nothing and have nothing to communicate. God gives it to us so we can communicate the gospel. It is spiritual power, boldness, not fear and timidity. It is the power to love others and keep on loving them. It is the power to give direction to our own lives. All of this we desperately need and humbly pray for. The vessel is empty if it is not filled with these gifts of God. So we are utterly dependent upon God to give these gifts to us in ordination and to keep giving them to us as we continue our ministry.

A word needs to be said further about self-control or self-discipline. We ministers are the only unsupervised servants in existence. We are on our own. The session seldom attempts to give any direction to the minister. The congregation may want to do

FOR FURTHER CONSIDERATION

❖ Interview members of the committee on the ministry in your presbytery on what ordination means to them. Interview at least five other ministers in your presbytery.

❖ Read *A Handbook, for the Committee on the Ministry*, 1984. Although this booklet is prepared for use by the committee on the ministry, reading it will inform you further on the meaning of ordination and give you better ideas of what the committee on the ministry in your presbytery may expect of you.

❖ *Have you read?* If you did not it will benefit you to dig out the April issue of 1991 of *The Cumberland Presbyterian* and read two articles: "Listening to the Darkness," Deborah Smith Douglas, and "The Shrinking Clergy Population," Barry Anderson. And further, read or re-read the issue of October 15, 1989, which highlights "Louisa Woosley: A First in American Presbyterianism, 100 Years Ago."

---

[16] II Timothy 1:6, 7.

so at times, but hesitates to do it. Consequently, we often get careless and lazy. We need the spirit of self-discipline God offers us. We must open our lives to it daily. It will enable us to do our work well. If God gives us the spirit of love and power, we will be able to continue without letting the demands of our calling burn us out.

Ordination certainly has more meanings than have been presented here, but let these suffice for the present. Much more can be learned about ordination as you prepare yourself for it.

When you are ordained, you are asked a number of questions by the committee on the ministry, and perhaps examined by the presbytery. In getting prepared to enter fully into the meaning of ordination read Section 6.30 "Ordination of Ministers" in the *Confession of Faith*, Constitution, pages 48-51. Set your mind to answer the questions you will be asked with honesty and sincerity. Deal openly with any problems you have with any questions you will be asked and with any matters of doctrine and polity which trouble you. This will enable you to be true to the promises and commitments you make. Don't make a mockery of your ordination by harboring any reservations with the intention of acting independently in some areas of church doctrine or polity. It will cause you trouble later and perhaps harm others.

It is hoped that this treatment of the theme of ordination will have led you to regard the ceremony in the light of its deeper meanings and prevent your wanting to rush into it without due preparation.

 CHAPTER 3

Ministry in the Small Church

THE PURPOSE OF THIS CHAPTER

This chapter is written for both laity and clergy who are serving, or will serve in small membership congregations.

The small church is different. The dynamics at work in it vary from those in larger membership congregations. It is essential to understand its nature, if one is to minister effectively in it.

This chapter is written as a very brief and simple introduction to the subject. It lays no claim to being anything more than a beginning. If it illuminates the nature of the small church and stimulates further study about it, it will have fulfilled its purpose.

THE SMALL CHURCH IS LEGITIMATE

Legitimate means lawful, legal, genuine, logical, justifiable.

It is often felt that to be small is to be worthless. Sometimes apologies are made for smallness. For instance, one may mention one's church hesitantly, saying, "Our church is just a small congregation," as if it were something of which to be ashamed. Those of us who grew up in, or belong to, small congregations may have felt the same way. To many of us small is bad; large is good. It is as if the small church is a failure, or that it is sick; or that it does not amount to very much.

In fact, many people do look down on the small church, and do not want to belong to one. They seek the status, and often the anonymity, of the large parish with multiple staff, and "Dr. So-and-So" as pastor.

The same feeling of inferiority regarding the small flock, may be experienced in belonging to a small membership denomination such as the Cumberland Presbyterian Church. The attitude may be that "small" means "bad," "sick," "useless," "ineffective," or "ugly."

Let us deny the validity of this attitude and declare the legitimacy and worth of the small membership church. The truth about this kind of church may appear more clearly as we further consider its characteristics.

It is not our purpose to set the small church against the larger one and claim exclusive value for it. We are only interested in making it clear that small membership congregations have a legitimate claim to worth as places of service. Both the small and the large parish fulfill needed ministry, though they are different in structure, nature, and their manner of administration.

SHOULD THE SMALL CHURCH GROW?

It is not to be assumed that in order for the reign of God to be fulfilled, small churches have to become larger. Some may; some may not. Some will; some will not. Some should; some should not. However, if a small church does become a large one, its character will change along with its way of ministry.

Many factors will contribute to growth, or the lack of it. Some small churches can grow. Others are in situations where growth is impossible. Some small churches will become smaller and finally die.

It is not our purpose to deal with such matters here. Our intention is to seek to understand more fully the nature of the small church.

A DENOMINATION OF SMALL CHURCHES

We can find some rationale for this search by realizing that the Cumberland Presbyterian denomination has more small churches than large ones. This must be taken into account by all who serve in them and who provide, plan, or select program and materials for them.

One statistical report has indicated that our denomination has 450 congregations with fewer than 100 members; that it has 100 congregations with between 40 and 60 members; and that there are 300 congregations with fewer than 40 members. These figures jolt us to the awareness that we must come to understand these churches, to learn better how to serve them, and to serve more effectively through them.

WHAT IS A SMALL CHURCH?

In some established denominations there seems to be a common agreement that a congregation of fewer than 200 members is to be considered a small church. On the other hand, Dr. Lyle Schaller, a professional in church planning and administration, suggests that any church that has an average attendance on Sunday of fewer than 45 to be considered a small church. Cumberland Presbyterian measurement has still another standard. Generally, we consider a church of 100-or-fewer members to be a small church. However, size is only one of many factors to take into account.

SOME CHARACTERISTICS OF THE SMALL CHURCH

1. *The small church is not so much an organization, as it is an organism*. It is more of a system, *like a family*. It concerns itself more with relationships than with organization and program. It tends to respond more to needs as they arise than to plan ahead. It is less mechanical, and more personal in its attitudes and actions.

This is in contrast to larger congregations and the ways they function. We cannot say that the small church is more spiritual or more Christian. It acts according to its character. There is great value, however, in its family-like personality. These facts call for a style of ministry better suited for a household than a corporation.

2. The small church is *usually limited in resources and programs*. Its economic base is weak because there are fewer people who can contribute. Small churches are often located in economically depressed areas. Inflation in recent years has caused dollars to buy less. This is felt keenly in small groups. They have difficulty in paying adequate salaries for pastoral services, and for support of programs. Personnel in adequate numbers are not available. It is often difficult even to find teachers for the church school. Nor does formal programming always fit the nature of the small congregation.

In spite of the lack of financial resources, adequate money seems always available for recognized and emergency needs. People tend to give to projects which are visible and which originate within the group, rather than those proposed by leaders.

3. *Intimacy in relationships* characterizes the small church. The members live in each others' lives. Everyone knows everyone else, and their "business." They gossip about each other. Secrets are seldom hidden. Members are "close" to each other and experience each others' lives and events personally. They share deeply in each others' pain and joy. They are neighborly and helpful.

4. In the small church, there is a *sense of ownership,* a sense of belonging, a sense of its being *my* church, and of having a part in decision-making. People have invested themselves and their money, and they feel the church is theirs.

This feeling is not always dependent upon formal membership. Some who have been adopted, or have adopted themselves, into the congregation without having taken church vows, come to feel that it is their church, too. They usually share their service and substance.

We see this sense of ownership as an asset and a strength.

5. *Decision-making is less formal than in larger churches.* Often, decisions are made unilaterally by individuals or groups without consultation with church officers or designated leaders. Sometimes it is difficult for the pastor and session to function officially. Tradition and custom, precedence and past practice, often dictate direction.

In one church two persons decided on their own to purchase a number of hymnals which cost a few hundred dollars. They evidently felt they had the right to do so. In another situation, even after the session had attempted to become the decision-maker, some small groups continued to act independently. It takes time, tact and patience to change such patterns.

6. *Communication is rapid and fairly complete* in the small church. Everyone knows what is going on. The word gets around fast. Personal contacts are more frequent. The telephone network stays active.

7. *Small churches are tough and tenacious.* They do not grow easily in most cases; nor do they die easily. They seem to maintain themselves at about the same level against great odds. In spite of few births, and frequent deaths, they maintain the status quo over long periods. Often they are survival-conscious, and worry about the future; but at the same time find it difficult to initiate plans for growth. Just how this stability in membership is maintained is a source of wonder, and

challenges us to investigate its cause.

8. *The small church wants to maintain its identity* regardless of its size and limitations. In this sense it is often stubbornly independent. Efforts on the part of presbytery to group it, or to encourage cooperation with similar congregations, or to unify resources, often fail.

Its roots sink deep and its history is preserved. It has a strong sense of who it is. The people feel planted in the past. They go "way back." They are "rooted and grounded" in their story. The world changes, and would change them, but they change little.

Related to this fact is their sense of "place."[1] Longtime associations and experiences where they are located makes the place sacred. Their church is a place "in the heart." They do not want to leave it. They may be settled in an inconvenient spot, off the beaten path because of community changes, or wed to a cemetery no longer easily available, yet they do not want to move. Tradition seems to be more valuable than growth.

This, too, has values beyond comprehension, in spite of the fact that it seems to fly in the face of success.

9. In smaller churches, *interactions among the people are different.* Structure is different. The dynamics are different.

The word "dynamics" refers to the various forces at work in any field. In the church it refers to the psychological, physical, geographical, environmental, moral, spiritual and mental energy at work there. Because of size, and other factors, this is different in a small church.

Hence, ministry is different. To succeed as a minister in a small church does not guarantee success in a larger one; nor are small churches good training grounds for ministry in larger ones, as is sometimes assumed.

10. *The small church does not fit the model for organizational efficiency.* In fact, efforts to be organized are resisted. It often operates better as a whole rather than through parts, such as task forces and committees. In this matter, it acts like a family. Families do not appoint committees. They decide and act in unity. To people in the small congregation, structured organization seems to too mechanical, superficial, and unnatural. They feel that some things may happen on their own, if given enough time and freedom, without manipulation or interference. Because of these feelings, the session may even find it hard to function as the decision-maker.

In spite of these facts, some organization is essential and should be encouraged. It is possible to set up some structures which are compatible with the principle of wholeness and unity. One church, rather than having all the committees usually recommended, has put together a council which cares for all concerns. Members of the session, as well as members from the congregation, are a part of this group. They are amenable to the session.

11. *The small church can be quick in response* because it does not deal in red tape. People can express their opinions openly on the spot. This has its advantages and disadvantages. One of the benefits is that needs can be cared for quickly without having to go through too many channels.

The opposite to this fast response is the fact that the small church can also

---

[1] *Making the Small Church Effective*, Carl Dudley, Abingdon Press, Chapter 6.

be, and often is, slow in response if you try to change too much too soon, or sometimes, if you try to change *anything*.

12. *Participation in the small church is high and it includes all generations.* In worship, for example, as well as in other programs and events, usually almost everyone is present, including the youngest to the oldest, and all of them can participate in some way or other. This is a beautiful and meaningful value.

13. *Contributions in the small church are higher per capita.* Necessity and visibility often make this true. But also, people invest in what they have a part in. They do not give by plan or pledge, but by need. They believe the money will come if the need is there. They initiate a project (like adding an addition to the building, erecting a manse, roofing the church, helping the needy, etc.) believing the money will be given. Often they do not first raise the money and then begin the undertaking. There is a value in this opportunity for spontaneous action in giving. The small church encourages spontaneity in other ways also. Giving from the heart has its values.

14. *Spiritual values are more easily obtainable in small churches.* This may be taken as a prejudicial statement by some. We believe it is true. It is probably true also for small groups within larger congregations.

We can assume that this is true because of the close and intimate relationships. Christian norms are communicated non-verbally through relationships more effectively even than formal teaching. The small congregation is like a family. People learn values by observing them as they are recognized in action by members of the group. This is more observable in small clusters. Closer relationships enhance the emotional attachments making for deeper impressions. Unconsciously people model for each other. The effect is strong.

In a homecoming event in a certain small church, the people were given an opportunity to tell what the church had meant to them. Without exception, though many had ranged far and wide in travel and experience, they testified how the seed of their faith had been planted there and the direction of their lives fairly well set. Many mentioned persons who had been big influences on them. These role models probably were like Moses, who "did not know the skin of his face shone because he had been talking with God."[2]

15. *Small churches do not grow quickly or easily.* (Some reference has been made to this fact in item 7.) People are slow to accept newcomers. They are reluctant to disturb the relationships in the group. They may like to have more people, if this were possible without too much change. They like things as they are. That is one reason they belong to the church. They seem to favor nothing which will upset status, position, power or communication.

Larger churches are more conditioned to growth and change; and can adapt to it. Smaller ones find it hard. Church growth methods, if effective, have to be adapted to the characteristics and attitudes of the small congregation.

16. *Formal church membership is not valued as highly as in larger churches.* In interviews with pastors it has been discovered that in practically every parish of limited membership, there are a few people who are definitely a part of the group, though they have never taken their church vows. (See item 4). This frustrates most pastors. They have tried to influence these persons toward formal

---

[2] Exodus 34:29.

membership; they have failed in most cases. Some of them have never made a profession of faith. Yet they attend and contribute.

Members of the churches do not seem to be troubled with this. Pastors wonder about the spiritual status of such persons, and feel they ought to do something about it.

What course should be pursued with regard to this matter?

17. *Traditional practices do not change easily in the small church.* Perhaps this is true also of larger churches in some situations. Probably it depends upon the size of the community and the culture of the area. However, it seems to be more true of the limited membership group.

Decisions are often made on precedent and custom. Tradition influences the nature of the group's life. It is the source of stability. In "The Fiddler on the Roof," Tevye says that everyone in the village is a fiddler on the roof. "And how do we keep our balance?" he asks. "Tradition!" he sings. Change brings uncertainty. Tradition gives security. Tradition has its values. Traditionalism (excessive respect for tradition) hinders progress.

In small churches things are done as they have always been done. Songs are sung which have always been sung. Try to change the music, try to introduce new ways of working, even approve rules making changes official, turn your head, and presto, things fall back into the rut, that good old comfortable rut.

As we have indicated, some of this is good. People know who they are by their traditions. But when tradition becomes traditionalism, and we live with our faces turned backward, we stumble into the present and future.

But don't change too quickly or too much; and don't expect the people to forsake the past to any great degree. Yet, with patience, tact and wisdom, changes can be made which are essential to spiritual growth and health.

18. In spite of what has been said, *small churches can be led.* They can be led into better worship, Christian education, leadership, service and mission. A good, trusting pastoral relationship will enhance the possibility. In any case the process will move slowly. It is essential to enable the people to take the lead, and to let them have a big part in making decisions.

Perhaps, in spite of traditionalism, and set ways, people consciously or unconsciously, expect, or want us to lead them, as reluctant as they are to follow.

19. *Small churches want to be loved.*

> The small church is built around the relationship of people to people. They want to know the pastor as a person, first. Only second are they interested in the pastor's skills...The pastor...is a source of stability, a kind of human blarney stone. There is no substitute for the presence of the pastor. He or she is the tangible symbol of love...[3]

If pastors become too "professional," put more emphasis on programming than relationships, they lose touch with what the people really want, and their effectiveness will decline.

For example, observation of a particular church exhibits the difference in pastoral styles between the pastor and the predecessor. One pastor was more or less a programmer. He wanted to help the "church be the church," and get involved in many concerns. He did well, but the response was less than he had hoped for.

---

[3] Ibid. Page 92.

His successor was different. He came loving, caring, relating. Over a period of time the people responded to him more warmly than to his predecessor.

20. *Leadership in the small church often becomes entrenched.* Seldom will the small parish have a rotating session. Often there are not enough replacements. Also, there is a tendency on the part of some elders to hold on to power.

Sometimes the congregation is "run" by a family, or an "in group." Usually these are represented on the session. Such persons are the "movers and shakers," or often the "non-movers and the non-shakers," for they want to maintain the status quo. Session meetings are often dominated by those who have caucused in preparation for a vote on issues. Perhaps a mixture of motives causes this. In some cases, those in power feel they are acting on behalf of the best interests of the people.

This situation may continue over a long period of time whether the members want it or not. It is the source of a great deal of frustration on the part of the pastor, for it is a hard problem to solve.

How would you go about achieving a balance of representation in the session and congregation?

IN REVIEW

A review of these traits of the small membership congregation will demonstrate that there are strengths and weaknesses, assets and debits. Working in this kind of situation is a challenge; and to some, a true joy. There are many positive values in such a situation which serve us well in our complicated and impersonal world. It is important that we learn better how to serve there, and lead the small church to realize its potential.

What other characteristics of the small church would you add?

A VISION OF SOMETHING BETTER FOR THE SMALL CHURCH

In spite of what has been said about the nature of the small church, some of which seems to be negative, we can have hope of improving ministry there. The following statement may improve our vision.

"A VISION OF A HEALTHY SMALL CHURCH"[4]

A small membership congregation is healthy
    when it has a sense of adventure and curiosity,
        and a desire to mature spiritually;
    when it measures the effectiveness of its life
        by its vision,
        and its witness to the Gospel,
    and when the worship of God
        becomes its daily life.

---

[4] This statement was prepared for the 1989 Assembly of the PCUSA. Written initially by Presbyterian Fathers in Small Church Strategy, it was then refined in the light of comments and insights received around the country.

A small church is healthy
   when it listens and responds to the will of God
      revealed in scripture and guided by the Holy Spirit;
   when it celebrates its unique qualities
      as well as its connection with people everywhere;
   when its ministry comes from Christ our Sovereign and Savior,
      to help people discover their power
      strengthen their commitment
      and practice an all-inclusive love.

A healthy small church
   can celebrate its unique identity
   and face honestly its struggles for survival;
      it benefits from presbytery affirmation
      and pursues cooperative relationships,
      both denominational and ecumenical.

A small church is healthy
   when it encourages the spiritual growth
      and draws on the diverse gifts of its members,
      trains its leaders,
      encourages stewardship
      and accepts responsibility for its own particular
      mission.

A small membership congregation is healthy
   when it fosters hospitality
      reaches out to those who are hurting
   when it is open to a variety of models
      of pastoral leadership and care
   and is willing to make changes
      in ways that help it meet the needs of the people
      in worship, education, nurture, fellowship, evangelism and mission.

Some objectives for any small congregation may emerge from a study of the above "vision." It seems to be saying to us:
- Turn to face forward and outward
- Emphasize the spiritual
- Help it remember its mission
- Preach and teach the whole gospel of personal salvation, Christian growth, social responsibility, witness and mission
- Build on its strengths and uniqueness
- Get it into the mainstream of the church and life
- Enable lay people to serve
- Plan mission projects the people can see
- Make it aware of a variety of models for ministry.

ADDITIONAL IDEAS WITH IMPLICATIONS FOR MINISTRY IN THE SMALL CHURCH

The Community. Although there are some common characteristics of small congregations, they are all different. This difference prevents our planning in the same way for all of them. It suggests, too, that the differences must be taken into account in their ministry. For example, small churches in the country, small towns, and cities are in different types of communities, and reflect different opportunities for service and witness.

In all cases, communities are changing in one way or another. Some are being urbanized, some are losing residents, some are growing, some have a good number of new people moving in, some remain about as they are with old-time residents in the majority, and some are balanced between old time residents and newcomers.

Resources. We have already noted that small churches have limited resources. In many cases, however, there are more resources than we realize. Many congregations have enough money, skills, and understanding to meet their needs. They may need leaders to help develop confidence in their own ability and strength. Small does not always mean weak.

Mobility. As we have become more mobile and travel-conscious, and as weekend entertainment pulls more of us out of the community, attendance and participation are affected. The small church suffers more visibly because of this.

Rather than reacting negatively, we need to find positive ways of relating to the situation. On Sundays, many ministers recognize the absentees. They often call names of people who are traveling, or on vacation, as well as those who are ill. All these are remembered in prayer and thought and thus recognized as a part of the congregation, though elsewhere in body. This tends to maintain the unity and wholeness of the group.

Culture. Both lay and pastoral leaders need to be a part of the culture of the people whom they serve. A knowledge of the history of the group will move them in this direction. It will enable them to identify with the people and to appreciate the faith they have received. In most congregations there are those who are a storehouse of knowledge of the past. They are willing to share their knowledge. From time to time they should be given the opportunity to keep all members current with the lore of the flock. Homecomings are good times to do it.

Survival or Mission? Many small churches need to be moved from a survival to a mission awareness. Too many center on maintenance more than mission, survival more than service. They wonder, and ask periodically, just how long the group will exist. We should remind them that God calls people to witness and work, not to wallow in what was, or to live by fear.

Resident Pastors. Clergy need to live with the people they serve. The ideal is for every congregation to have a resident minister. In many cases this is not possible.

Ministers who live elsewhere and serve only on weekends need to do a lot of visiting when they are in the community and with the people. This will enable them to live to some extent in the lives of the people and serve their needs.

More Pastoral Service. Small churches need, and deserve, more pastoral service than they are receiving. Too many have only a part-time ministry by non-resident pastors. Presbytery Boards of Mission should concern themselves with this condition.

Vision. Small churches often need a wider vision of ministry. They sometimes do not see beyond their own community. Their sense of self-worth and ability to serve can be developed by leading them into a world vision and participation in world mission. A church is as big or as little as its vision. Its enthusiasm is also often affected by far or near-sightedness. Materials provided by our denominational boards are designed to open us to the world.

Self-Study. Some churches have found it beneficial to do a self-study. They use materials provided by the Cumberland Presbyterian Board of Missions. Some have used *Smaller Church Mission Study Guide* (Henry A. Blunk, The Geneva Press, 1978). It takes effort to prepare a congregation for this project. However, it may be the very best means for opening the door to the future. Presbytery boards of missions may be a source of help in this endeavor.

Models For Ministry. Here follows a number of models. The model needs to be fitted with the situation.[5]

A VARIETY OF MODELS FOR PASTORAL LEADERSHIP AND CARE

1. *Solo Pastorate*—One pastor serves a single field full-time. Church provides full financial support for the pastor.

2. *Yoked Field*—Two churches share a pastor, the churches joining together at least in part to provide a more solid base of financial support for securing longer term, full-time pastoral leadership.

3. *Area Ministry*—Regional grouping of churches with one full-time pastor who is a member of the presbytery staff, and is appointed as stated supply for the churches, and works with lay preachers and other staff for support and development of the churches. Financial support for the ministry is shared by presbytery, synod, and the churches.

4. *Larger Parish*—More than two churches sharing a single full-time pastor, plus other part-time staff for worship leadership. Again, sharing by the churches helps provide a financial basis for pastoral leadership.

5. *Solo Field, part-time position*—A church seeks a pastor to serve part-time…retired pastor or tentmaking pastorate (see below).

6. *Tentmaking pastorate*—Pastor is hired to serve a church part-time and, with areas of responsibility agreed to by all, also has secular employment. This model of providing pastoral leadership is receiving increased attention in the Presbyterian Church (USA). [This is also true of the Cumberland Presbyterian church.]

7. *Pastor Shared with Presbytery* (The Greenbrier Model)—Pastor serves a congregation on a part-time basis and the rest of the time on presbytery (or synod) staff. Financial support is shared by the congregation and presbytery.

8. *Seminary Student Pastor*—A seminary student serves the church, regularly leading Sunday worship and performing other pastoral functions, largely on weekends. Presbytery appoints an ordained minister as moderator of the session.

9. *Clergy Couple*—A couple is called to serve one or more churches. A variety of arrangements are possible for full or part-time ministry among the participating churches.

10. *Lay Preacher/Stated Supply*—A congregation is served week to week by a duly appointed lay preacher; a Stated Supply moderates session meetings and administers the sacraments in accord with Presbytery and session agreement.

11. *Ecumenical Parish*—A pastor is supported by two or more denominations

---

[5] These models emerged from a discussion in a Small Church Conference in Kiskiminetas Presbytery, PCUSA, 1989. Used by permission.

cooperating on the call. The arrangement may be a federated church (sharing a common building but maintaining their own denominational rolls and rotating the pastoral call among the participating denominations of a yoked field.)

12. *Minister-at-large*—An experienced pastor serves on the presbytery staff and works on contract with a local congregation, providing pastoral services, program and administrative leadership, while the congregation works towards specific goals, resolves issues, or discerns how it best can secure long term pastoral leadership for the future.

13. *Satellite Relationship*—A smaller congregation relates to a larger church, and shares the support for services of the pastor, or from an additional staff member of the larger congregation.

This chapter on the small church is a mere introduction, and lays no claim to be a full treatment of the subject. The books listed below offer a way for further learnings in this field.

FOR FURTHER READING AND STUDY

Making the Small Church Effective, Carl S. Dudley, Abingdon, 1978, 192 pages. The statement on the back of the paperback indicates something about the content and flavor of the publication:

> In a big world, the small church has remained INTIMATE. In a fast world, the small church has been STEADY. In an expensive world, the small church has remained PLAIN. In a complex world, the small church has remained SIMPLE. In a rational world, the small has kept FEELING. In a mobile world, the small church has been an ANCHOR. In an anonymous world, the small church CALLS US BY NAME.

Unique Dynamics of the Small Church, Carl S. Dudley, The Alban Institute, Inc., 1977. Reprinted 1984, 1988. This is a small paperback booklet of 21 pages.

Entering the World of the Small Church, Anthony G. Pappas, The Alban Institute, 1988, 93 pages.

Developing Your Small Church's Potential, Carl S. Dudley, Douglas Alan Walrath, Judson Press, 1988, 96 pages.

Christian Education in the Small Church, Donald L. Griggs, Judy McKay Walther, Douglas Alan Walrath, editor. Judson Press, 1988, 112 pages.

Planning for Your Church, Douglas A. Walrath, Westminster Press, 1984, 112 pages.

"The Gap: Is There Division Between Urban and Rural Church People?," *The Cumberland Presbyterian*, January 1991 (vol. 163, no. 1).

 CHAPTER 4

The Pastoral Relationship

The purpose of this Chapter is to help the reader understand the nature of the pastoral ministry. It will not provide guidance on *how* to do pastoral work. That will come later.

Ministry in and with a congregation has to do with relationships. It is a relationship of the pastor with the people as a whole, and with individuals; not just a relationship to an institution. Our *Confession of Faith* uses the words *relation* and *relationship* in referring to this association.[1] Normally, a bonding develops over a period of time, and mutual experience; and is built on trust, responsibility, commitment, loving and caring.

Pastors are not employed as hired persons. They are joined as equal partners with a congregation. They are not contracted with as a manager to run the show, or merely to do a job. They have been invited to share their lives with a church and a community. Although they are expected to do the work of ministry, their true vocation is to love.

The pastoral role allows one "to personalize the Gospel in an impersonal world, and to affirm people as children of God, each with his or her own uniqueness."[2]

Nothing in the ministry is more important than the pastoral relationship. Everything else is built upon it.

A BIBLICAL MODEL FOR PASTORAL CARE

No technical description of pastoral functions will suffice. Although there are methods involved in pastoral work, technical language cannot grasp, or fully express, the nature of the pastoral relationship. It is too cold and mechanical. Nor will prose serve as an adequate channel for communicating the pastoral concept. It is too wooden.

---

[1] *Confession of Faith*, Constitution, 1984, Section 7.00, pages 53-55.

[2] *The Rebirth of Ministry*, James D. Smart, Westminster Press, 1960, 192 pages, Chapter 5, "The Minister as Pastor"

Only poetic language will do when we talk about the minister as pastor. That is because poetry has to do with feelings, insights and the intangibles of imagination and spirit. This language fits the pastoral theme for pastoring deals with warm bodies and living souls: sensitive, vulnerable, and delicate.

Biblical language is, to a great extent, poetic; and uses metaphors, images and symbols to convey its message. That is the reason we turn to the Bible to help us understand pastoral ministry.

The 23rd Psalm, a Psalm of David, is an example. It was written by a "man after God's own heart"[3] who had been a shepherd. David used the image of the shepherd to show how God cares for us. The shepherd is an excellent image for the pastoral relationship. The shepherd gives unmeasured love to the sheep. So does the good pastor. The pastor does not calculate how much to give, nor count hours; but loves without fear of what it will cost. This is the way God is. This is the way a good pastor is, too.

Let us see what this image of God as the good shepherd says to us as pastors. (Vs. 1)

The herdsman the Psalmist had in mind is the Palestinian shepherd. Shepherding in that rugged, arid land was hard work. It was difficult to find green pastures and cool water in that land. These had to be sought diligently. However, the faithful shepherd never despaired. His sheep had to be fed and watered, and he alone was responsible.

When it is written that *the shepherd made the sheep to lie down in green pastures*, it meant he had found a green spot in a desertland for them to feed upon. The sheep were able to do this in a relaxed manner in a dangerous territory, as the words "lie down" suggest. (vs. 2)

The good pastor searches for food for his/her people in a sparse land today. The major task is to feed the flock, to satisfy their hunger for love, truth and reality. (The word "pastor" comes from a Latin word, "pascere", meaning "to feed.") This task takes searching, and is suggestive of the kind of discipline pastoring requires. *The green pastures are the Word of God found in the Scriptures.*[4]

Let us stop for a moment to think of the nature of sheep as indicative of the nature of the people in our fold. Sheep are members of a flock. They exist as separate, individual animals, each with its own needs and nature; but, they as individuals always exist in relation to other sheep in a herd. Sheep, also, tend to follow each other, for good or evil.[5]

People, individually, in relation to other people, are the concern of the pastor who deals with them as individuals, but always as in relation to others, such as: the family, the congregation, the state, the nation, and the world. Our relationships, especially those in the family, make us what we become.

The good shepherd leads his flock to a quiet place for water. (Vs. 2b) Water is doubly important in a desert. It is essential to life. It is not easy to find in a dry land. So what does the shepherd do? He finds a little stream, dams it, and lets the water back up to form a quiet pool. Sheep will not drink from a turbulent stream. Here in a secluded spot, but still in threatening surroundings, the sheep drink from quiet

---

[3] I Samuel 13:14

[4] II Timothy 2:15

[5] Isaiah 53:6

waters.

The pastor finds water as well as food for the people of his flock. The quiet water from which they are to drink is Jesus Christ. He is, as he claimed, the Living Water. Nothing can be substituted for him. The social sciences of the day are good resources for the care of souls and should be utilized for ministry, but the core of our need is Jesus Christ. Nothing, and no one else, can satisfy our thirst. We may be very adept in "handling" people, and we may become skillful in using methods to move people through crises, and enabling them to find themselves, but most of all they need to find, or to be found by, Jesus Christ. It is ours to bring them together into a redeeming relationship.

David writes that the good shepherd restores his soul. (Vs. 3) This follows the words about green pastures and still waters. Does it suggest that when we have the right sustenance there is a sense of becoming whole, or being healed and restored to completeness?

Or do these words suggest that the soul can be stolen, and Jesus Christ brings it back? Can the world rob us of our true being and substitute something false instead? Can the true self be lost? Can we be hoodwinked into striking bargains—our souls for some cherished status, power, or possession? And is Jesus Christ the one to get it back for us?

(Soul is being used as the true self. We do not believe in a soul separate from our whole being. We do not have souls—we *are* souls.)

Or, further, does verse 3 say that life sometimes just wears us down, bruises us, disorients us, wounds us, threatens to destroy us; and that we limp along on crutches, which are poor makeshifts for the real thing? And, that Jesus Christ heals us?

We pastors must minister Christ to those who are wounded and hurting. "A bruised reed he will not break, and a dimly burning wick he will not quench."[6]

The good shepherd leads his flock. He does not drive them. He goes before them. (Vs. 3b) His visible presence reassures them. They tend to go where he is. He draws them. He breaks new paths for them. He pioneers. He pushes back the frontier. They respond to his leading for they trust him.

He leads them in "paths of righteousness." This is one of those terms which is vague, general, and hard to define. Does righteousness mean morality? Right conduct? Justice? Virtue? Yes, when defined in the light of relationships.

Would not rightness be the proper definition? Rightness which means fitting? In this sense, rightness in relationships; rightness in relation to God and others. A rightness which means fitting to our nature and the nature of God; and a rightness with nature which is fitting to our responsibility? Does it mean Jesus sets us right, puts us into the proper position with relation to all of life? And is not the feeling we have at times that everything is right indicative that it really is? How peaceful it is to feel right with God, right with ourselves, and right with other people! How terrible when we are not!

The shepherd leads in paths of righteousness "for his name's sake." In the Bible a name does not only distinguish a person from another, but has to do with the nature of the person. The good shepherd leads in paths of righteousness because it is his nature to do so. These paths are according to our true nature also, and to

---

[6] Isaiah 42:3

depart from them is to go against the way God has made us. Jesus Christ enables us to become what God intended for us to become. The kingdom of God is realism. It fits our nature and fulfills us. In the light of this conviction, pastors can carry on their work with assurance.

Good pastors lead; they do not push. They lead the people into new pathways which are right ways. They lead by what they are more than by what they know or say. They lead by their own nature, as ones who have, in their experience of God, earned their own right to lead. They do not lead by autocratic direction. They lead through character and influence. Skills and methods of leadership are essential, but they are secondary.

Good pastors lead; they do not follow. Some people-pleasing pastors test the winds of opinion and go where they are blown. Sometimes they are very "successful" by some standards. The true pastor leads. Leadership is a very draining and dangerous work. It demands faith, confidence, courage, commitment, tact, insight, thoughtfulness, and just plain guts. What will happen if the pastor does not lead?[8]

In verse 4, David expresses his own sense of security even in the darkest hours of his life because he knows God is near. "The valley of the shadow of death" has been interpreted in several ways. One is that death is only a shadow. That is not so. Death is a reality. This phrase is a figure of speech denoting a dark and threatening experience of some kind. It can mean a relentless temptation, fear and anxiety, failure, tragedy, loss, sorrow, danger, depression (the valley), and discouragement.

Good pastors walk through the valley of the shadow with the flock, are there for them, and see them through the crisis. Although ministers are wordsmiths, there are times when words are not the need. Presence is. The presence of the pastor is the presence of God, the pastor being the symbol of God's presence and love. Just to be there is the essence; just to be there at the right time.

(Lest it may seem that only the ordained clergy are deemed pastors, let it be said again that the interpretation of pastoral care and presence given here includes the laity; in fact, it intends to emphasize the laity.)

Verse 4 has two metaphors which should not be overlooked. They are the rod, and the staff. The rod was a club, probably shaped from a sapling by the shepherd's digging it up, trimming its roots down, leaving some spike-like prongs, and cutting it off to a length of two or three feet. He used this to fight off wild animals which sometimes attacked the sheep. The shepherd was a "protector and defender" of the flock. He had courage and learned how to do battle with dangerous foes. In this sense, he was like Samson, no mere stripling, but a rugged man of the out-of-doors.

Some of these same qualities are desirable in any caregiver. The pastor is to be the protector of the flock, a fighter, who sees the danger and attacks the enemy which would destroy it. There are many forces which attack today. The challenge calls not only for courage and strength, but skill in spiritual warfare. The whole church is involved in this conflict.[9]

---

[7] Ephesians 2:13-22

[8] I Corinthians 14:8

[9] Ephesians 6:19, 20

The shepherd not only had a rod; *he also had a staff*. This staff was a large slender stick or pole about an inch or more in diameter with a crook at one end, formed into a kind of semicircle, which was shaped while the wood was still green. It is referred to at times as the shepherd's crook. He used this to help himself walk over rough terrain; but its main purpose was to rescue lost sheep.

When a sheep had wandered off, being lured by one green tuft after another, or following another stray, and perhaps falling down the side of a hill, or into a crevice, the shepherd could extend the staff downward, maneuver the crook around its body, and lift it out.

The staff is a symbol of the seeking and rescuing pastor-shepherd. The pastor is interested in saving lost sheep. She or he seeks them at great risk; and at great effort, rescues them and restores them to the fold.

"Thy rod and thy staff, they comfort me." (Vs. 4) *Pastors are to comfort the people;* which means reassuring them and showing compassion to them. Comfort means, though, more than being patted on the back and told that everything is going to turn out all right. The English word *Comfort* comes from a Low Latin word meaning *to make strong*. So the word means *strength*. We are strengthened by Christ's being with us, and we with him. When we comfort someone we give them strength by being with them as Christ's representative. Thus we are Christs to each other (Luther). We give strength, rather than letting them feel sorry for themselves, the most debilitating attitude anyone can assume.

In verse 5 the table spread in the presence of enemies suggests that *often pastoral care is given in the context of danger*. Although we need to be positive and emphasize the power of God in the world, we must also be realistic. There are evil forces in the world working to destroy the good. This view adds urgency to pastoral care.

"Thou anointest my head with oil" (Vs. 5b) is a metaphor which suggests another dimension to pastoral work. The image is of the shepherd standing at the gate of the fold at evening time, examining each animal for any wounds or abrasions it might have suffered during the day, and pouring oil into the injury to heal it.

There is not a single person who has not been, or will not be, wounded by life in some way. Glance over the congregation on any given Sunday and you will be aware that among many who are well, there are those who are hurting. Drive down the streets where the people live. You know some of them are in pain. *You are to be a healer as well as a proclaimer.*[10]

"My cup overflows. Surely goodness and mercy shall follow me all the days of my life..." (Vss. 5c and 6) *David is asserting a strongly positive attitude toward life.* He cannot contain or use all the goodness of life God has poured into him. God gives with an extravagance.

Often in Scripture, *the cup* refers to a hard or tragic experience. Here it means beneficence. Life is too good and rich to be contained in our little cups. In spite of bad things happening to us, God's grace overflows.

Do you ever feel this? Many people do not, and seemingly, cannot. Life appears to be too devastating for them. Fortunate are those for whom life is an overwhelming graciousness.

---

[10] Jeremiah 8:22

Verse 6 says something similar. To many people life is a negative existence. Ill fate dogs their tracks. Nothing good ever seems to come their way. On the contrary, here is David saying that goodness and love follow him wherever he goes. They seek him out and try to overfill his life with benefits.

How did David come by this attitude? He had experienced terrible times and troubles. Yet, somewhere along the way he had become aware of God's Providence which overrode everything else. To him this was not only true for this life, but for eternity. "And I shall dwell in the house of the Lord forever." (Vs. 6b)

Are we pastors not called to enable people to experience life as an overflowing cup?[11] *We want them to feel that God seeks them out to bless and save.* Attitudes are not easy to teach, or to learn. It is simpler to teach someone good behavior than good feeling. Perhaps the effective thing will be that we acquire that attitude ourselves. Good attitudes are contagious.

ANOTHER BIBLICAL MODEL FOR PASTORAL CARE

We will make a temporary digression from the shepherd model of ministry. Ezekiel is the watchman model. "Son of man, I have made you a watchman for the house of Israel; whenever you hear a word from my mouth, you shall give them a warning from me."[12] Ezekiel was a prophet rather than a pastor. However, there were pastoral potentialities in him. We will make a reference to one of them.

Read Ezekiel 3:12-15. God has spoken to Ezekiel about the attitudes and lives of the exiles to whom he was to minister. This had aroused Ezekiel's spirit and sent him with haste to speak to them and correct them. He seemed to be full of rage and of zeal for the Lord. "I went in bitterness in the heat of my spirit, the hand of the Lord being strong upon me." (Vs. 14)

When he arrived at the place the exiles were dwelling, Ezekiel stayed with them seven days. "I sat where they sat, and remained there astonished among them seven days." (Vs. 15 KJ) This means he experienced life fully with them, does it not? He saw with Monday's eyes, and heard with Tuesday's ears, and felt with Wednesday's fingers, and tasted with Thursday's tongue; he smelled with Friday's nose, and chilled with Saturday's body, and walked with Sunday's feet. He experienced a complete round of life with them. He was astonished by what he found out about them. Afterward his righteous indignation was tempered with mercy and understanding.

Ezekiel the *prophet* was moved by the prophet's rage and zeal. But Ezekiel the *shepherd* was touched by the people's condition, and came to feel with them. Only then was he able to preach the word effectively.

The pastor-shepherd, if he/she is to minister with compassion and understanding, must come to feel with the sheep, must sit where they sit for seven days. This identification with the people is absolutely essential to good pastoral care. There are those who tell you to maintain some distance between yourself and your parishioners. To an extent this may be true. We have to keep control of our feelings or be rendered helpless in emergencies. This does not mean, however, we are to have or show no feelings. How can a cold, unfeeling person pastor anyone?

---

[11] John 10:10

[12] Ezekiel 3:17

> Agonies are one of my changes of garments,
> I do not ask the wounded person how he feels,
> I myself become the wounded person,
> My hurts turn livid upon me as I lean on a
> cane and observe.[13]

"Rejoice with those who rejoice, weep with those who weep."[14]

To the Jews I became a Jew, in order to win Jews; to those under the law I became as one under the law—though not being myself under the law—that I might win those under the law. To those outside the law I became as one outside the law—not being without law toward God but under the law of Christ—that I might win those outside the law. To the weak I became weak, that I might win the weak. I have become all things to all people, that I might be all means save some.[15]

A THIRD MODEL FOR PASTORAL MINISTRY

We return to the shepherd model; the content of the material, however, will be somewhat different. Jesus describes himself as the good shepherd and points out the characteristics of a good shepherd as he relates to the sheep.[16]

The following quote gives emphasis to the meaning of the shepherd model for ministry.

> The shepherd image of ministry is woven throughout the fabric of Scripture and in the historical witness of the church. The scrapes and scraps of human flesh and toil are many. They need attention if the world is to reach the wholeness God intended for his creation. It is the work of the shepherd to pay attention. To be with. To love. To truly care for the flock. Imagine baptism without touching. Imagine teaching or preaching without first 'hearing with their ears.' Imagine feeding without 'suffering with their spirit.' Imagine tending without loving and helping and healing. Jesus did all those things. The main model for ministry is Jesus himself.[17]

John 10:1-18 says very much the same thing as Psalm 23, with some exceptions. However, there is a difference in the two passages due to the fact that David wrote the Psalm and John's passage are the words of Jesus. What was said about the Lord being our shepherd in Psalm 23 was actually fulfilled in Jesus Christ. He modeled and lived it out in his life and ministry. Jesus not only said he was the good shepherd, he actually was, and is; for in the Holy Spirit he continues to do his shepherding work. He also does it through those who are chosen as shepherd-pastors.

---

[13] Walt Whitman, Song of Myself, 1855

[14] Romans 12:15

[15] I Corinthians 9:20-22

[16] John 10:1-18

[17] *The First Parish*, J. Keith Cook, Westminster Press, 1983, 154 pages. See page 10.

As the good shepherd, Jesus had an intimate relation with the sheep. He knew them by name. He called them out one at a time to follow. They recognized his voice and trusted him. They would not follow a stranger, for they did not know his voice. There was a communication between the sheep and the shepherd. There still is. To be Christian is to have this intimate and real relationship with Jesus.

As the good shepherd, Jesus led the sheep out, out of the fold into a life outside, to help them find food and water and fulfillment.[18]

As the good shepherd, Jesus gave his life to and for the sheep. The shepherd lives for the sheep; that is his purpose for being. Every day he gives a part of himself to them. Jesus still does. The climax of Jesus' life was on the cross, which is both a symbol and a fact. It is a symbol of his commitment to us forever. He never leaves or forsakes us.

As the good shepherd, Jesus is not a hireling who is paid to herd the sheep, but has no love for them. The hireling runs when there is danger and leaves the sheep to themselves. Jesus contrasts himself with some religious leaders who are motivated for gain, not love.

As the good shepherd, Jesus has a sense of being loved and approved by God. "The Father loves me, because I lay down my life, that I may take it up again." (Vs. 17) Self-sacrifice kindles love in God's heart.

As the good shepherd, Jesus gives his life on his own. No one forces him. He is free to lay it down or to pick it up. "I lay it down on my own accord." (Vs. 18) He is inner motivated and self-motivated. Nothing outside himself forces or influences him to give: not reward, not status, not approval, and not acclaim.

As the good shepherd, Jesus has an imperative to bring others into the fold. This is one of the sometimes-mentioned "musts" of Jesus. "Them I *must* bring." (Vs. 16 KJ) This is an inner sense of urgency and necessity. Jesus seemed to place an unusual premium on lost sheep. In the parable[19] the shepherd leaves the 99 sheep in the fold to seek the one that was lost. He never gave up. He sought "until" he had found it; which indicates the strength of the imperative to bring the lost into the fold. When the lost sheep had been found there was great rejoicing.

As the good shepherd, Jesus sought for unity. "So there shall be one flock, one shepherd." (Vs. 16) Sheep are not to exist alone. They cannot endure alone. They need the flock. They are made for community. Their individuality is conditioned by the group. They are one of many. Jesus sought for wholeness, completeness and harmony.

Jesus is our model.

The models for ministry above stressed certain implications for our shepherding work.[20] There are additional implications to be found in the John 10:1-18 model. We add them to the others in the paragraphs below.

---

[18] Isaiah 40;11

[19] Luke 15:3-7

[20] Psalm 23 and Ezekiel 3:12-15

MORE IMPLICATIONS FOR PASTORAL MINISTRY FROM THE SHEPHERD MODEL

Good pastors are open, vulnerable, warm, friendly and outgoing. They come to know their people well and call them by name. The people should come to know the pastor well also. Openness on the pastor's part will help. It is difficult for some people to be open. They just do not want to get "close" to others. They hold themselves in reserve. They either fear to let people know them well lest they be rejected, or they simply are timid and slow to show feelings. People with poor self images do not want to be "found out," so they do not open up. It is difficult to shepherd people if there is not a mutual openness and communication. The pastor often has to take the lead in this area.

Personal relationships are enhanced if pastors identify themselves as full-fledged human beings. The "Messiah complex" often hinders some clergy. They put themselves too far above their people. People tend to revere, or idealize, the ordained minister. Some preachers like that, and encourage it. They like to be answer givers, rather than communicators.

Jesus became one with other human beings.[21] Good pastors never think of themselves as being above anyone. They are an integral part of everyday humanity. They have emptied themselves of pride and exaggerated self-importance.

There are walls built between people because of attitudes, culture, money, status, class and race. Some people are not comfortable in the presence of a minister because of these barriers. They are not comfortable in the presence of a pastor because of the pastor's education, attitudes, aura (just being a clergy person does it for some), speech, or dress. They feel the pastor is unapproachable.

It is important to break down walls and to bridge gaps. Just speaking to people in a friendly way will help. There are some persons to whom being spoken to is of ultimate importance and not being spoken to is the ultimate insult. They need to be recognized as persons and affirmed by a greeting. Ministers are symbols of the love and care of God. As such they minister to everyone, or fail to do so, whether they are in the church or not.

Good pastors are approachable. If ministers preach dogmatic and argumentative sermons, do not like to be challenged, and insist on their own way, people will hesitate to open up to them. If ministers take controversial stands on current issues in authoritarian ways, many will be alienated. If ministers appear to think too highly of themselves and are aloof, people react and put a distance between them.

A good rule to follow is to assume such an attitude in speech and manner that people will feel they can say anything to you without fear of being turned off. This should be done honestly; for who has all the answers, or knows the best, or sees all the truth? Don't let your intelligence, family, blood, heritage and training set you apart from common humanity. Keep remembering that you are just a human being, not a god or super man or woman. Your call and commitment to the ministry do not make you into a Messiah. As a human being you are no better or worse than anyone else. Humility invites and builds solid relationships.

Good pastors are available to people. Sometimes pastors unconsciously send

---

[21] Philippians 2:1-11 and Luke 3:21, 22

the message that they are too busy to be bothered. People pick up on these signals and stay away. They do not want to pester the pastor.

Keep your door open to people. Let them feel you have plenty of time for them and that each one of them is important. Remember you are here to communicate God's love. Everything you do enhances or hinders this purpose.

Of course, there are those who will "hog your time." They may have more needs than others; or think they have. They may have an exaggerated sense of their own importance. They may be in the habit of using others to their own purposes. Or, they may feel their position and status merit extra attention. Being open is a risk you run. You can learn to handle them in order to give others the time and attention they deserve.

All of this means that you cannot think of hours and workloads. Your days are not to be clocked, nor the hours counted. You are available to those in need. Any slight indication that people do not have access to you will close the door to them. Some professionals can do this, and perhaps should. They can say "Don't call me at night." You can't say that. Shepherding is not a profession. It is a calling.

Of course, pastors should have days off, and vacations, and have freedom for renewal.

Good pastors visit in the homes of the people insofar as it is possible. They need to make contact with the people on their own turf, where they are their "everyday" selves. Pastors thus come to know the people better, especially if on some of these occasions there is time enough for a meal or a relaxed call.

It may be helpful to assume that you do not really know a person, or a family, until you have been in their home. Seeing people at church, or making casual and superficial contact otherwise, are hardly enough to provide a more intimate knowledge and understanding of them.

Pastors have an amazing privilege which often is taken for granted. It is this. Most homes are open to the pastor. This liberty is shared almost exclusively with the doctor. This is a freedom not to be taken advantage of or passed off lightly. This fact may be less true in larger population centers, and maybe today, than a few years back; nevertheless in most of the communities and churches of our communion people welcome the pastor to their homes. Of course, with the increased activities engaging family members, and the fact that so many women work outside the home, the situation has been altered.

The matter of time for frequent visits has to be considered seriously. Some homes will not be open to you for various reasons. You will have to relate to these persons in some other way, such as, their place of work (briefly), on social occasions, on the street, at the post office and the like.

Some pastors print in their bulletins the names of families they would like to visit on any given week. Families have the privilege of cancelling or rearranging the time. Other pastors make known hours and days they are available for home visits and let the people determine if they want visits or not. Some pastors have such a relationship with the families in their churches that they can drop in often, sometimes, even without telephoning that they are coming.

A certain amount of chit-chat is carried on in pastoral visits, which often are social in nature, and have little to do with the church and religion. This is not wrong. People do not have to talk religion all the time. These occasions often afford opportunities for fact-finding about the family and its members.

Don't let your reluctance to visit (some pastors do not like to do it and others are not sure of themselves) or the difficulty of finding satisfactory ways of doing it, hinder you from this important activity. It is essential to the most productive pastoral care.

Here let it be said that if you do not care for people, or find it difficult to relate to them, or if you cannot accept them as they are, you need to consider a way other than pastoral work to express your calling. Or, possibly you can think of further education and training for the pastoral ministry.

Further, in this impersonal world, where people easily lose their identity, there is a need for affirmation of them as persons. Make every effort to meet their need by relating often to them; and take advantage of every chance contact you make with them which has not been planned. Sometimes these "accidental" meetings yield richly and prove to be God-given. One pastor complained he could not go to the post office and return on schedule without having to stop and talk to people on the street. He was blind to Providence.

One pastor did a lot of visiting, but he became disappointed. It did not seem to be yielding much fruit, especially in terms of church attendance. That suggests the question about the purpose of pastoral visits. The answer is that the major purpose is not to keep people loyal to the church. Some ministers have made it so. Some people may accept this. Though, it can turn off others. Visits and contacts are to be made out of concern for the welfare of the people, not primarily to build the institution. Even calls to evangelize should be pastoral.

We have been told that if a family misses church three times consecutively, the minister should check up on them. Why? To get them back to church? Not mainly. They should be visited to see if they have needs or problems that should be tended. Often they may say, "We are glad we were missed," and the visit will have affirmed their worth as persons. Sometimes they may say without prompting, "We know we must get back to church."

Good pastors also make visits to the sick and aged. These include those who are at home, in a hospital, or in a nursing home. All these need special care because their life situations have caused particular needs which demand attention and love. The aging and homebound need more care than they often receive. Some pastors shamefully neglect them to spend time with members who are more active. It is as if older and inactive members cease to be persons with needs when they can no longer do things for the church. Remember that many of these people carried the load when they were able. However, even though they may not have served well, they are children of God who need care. Our worth as persons does not depend on how well we can function; rather, it is based on our innate value as creatures of God. Even the least useful and most self-destructive person on earth deserves our love. The good shepherd never ceases to seek the lost, wounded or straying sheep.

The pastoral function of home visitation includes as many concerns as there are in the total ministry of Jesus Christ. The pastor may preach one to one (briefly) if the need is there; or teach and inform; or act as a priest in prayer; or counsel. At times he or she may evangelize, comfort and encourage. Thus pastoral ministry becomes a whole ministry.[22]

Good pastors learn to listen. They listen to the words of people as they share

---

[22] *The Rebirth of Ministry*, James D. Smart, Westminster, 1960 page 111, 112

themselves freely. They listen between the lines to see what is really being said. They listen to body language—body positions, movement of the hands, expressions on the face and in the eyes, and whether the body is tense or relaxed.

In learning to listen, pastors keep quiet and let others talk. This sometimes goes against the grain of habit; preachers often think they are to do all the talking. They may think they should cheer people up by amusing them with tales and jokes. May the Lord deliver us from perpetually joke-telling pastors!

Some pastors listen only to get a cue for some event or story they want to tell. Although everyone involved in a visit should have an opportunity to talk, the major intent of a pastoral visit is to listen to others, and encourage sharing on their part. A listening ear and a loving touch are worth more than all the sermons one may be. "Though I speak with the tongues of men and of angels."[23]

Cultivate the art of listening!

Good pastors reach outside the church. "Other sheep I have."[24] "The world is my parish."[25] It has been said that "the church exists for those outside its doors." Good pastors not only reach out beyond the church, but they teach their people to do so also. This proves to be a most difficult task in some cases, but is essential to growth and ministry.

The church either reaches out or it becomes a ghetto. Some churches have become ghettos. The "saved" huddle securely together, concerned only for themselves and their own. The pastor, as a kept person, ministers to them as their private chaplain. This is hardly what Jesus Christ intended when he commanded us to go into all the world.

Church membership not keeping up with population growth has made the church a minority institution. More people are being born than become members of the church. Further, there seem to be more people who feel themselves to be isolated, excluded or strangers to the body of believers. They may have a wrong conception of the nature of the church and therefore keep themselves out of it. On the other hand, the attitude of the church might be the cause. We in the church tend to be more adept at talking with each other than with those outside the fold. We tend to be at a loss when it comes to communicating with those who are not a part of our heritage. Also, many of us in the church seem to be totally indifferent to the evangelistic mission.

The pastor must reach out and call the people to follow. This demands constant and intentional evangelistic preaching and teaching.

Good pastors bring the presence and power of God to bear upon people's lives. The pastor is not just a public relator, trying to make friends of everyone; nor an administrator seeking support for programs; nor a soothsayer telling people what they want to hear. Nor is the pastor a psychologist or a psychiatrist applying the latest insights to his or her work.

It is tragic for pastors to forsake their major role to become self-styled psychiatrists. The increased emphasis on counseling over the years has misled many pastors. They have been hoodwinked into mistaking psychology for the gospel.

---

[23] I Corinthians 13:1 KJ

[24] John 10:16 KJ

[25] John Wesley

The pastor is a reconciler and needs an understanding of psychology; however, the pastor is not a minister of psychology, but of the gospel. The heights and depths of human nature can only be dealt with by God. The pastor is an instrument to this end.

Good pastors are community builders. They recognize that the church is the body of Christ, and to be true to its nature, must work harmoniously together. They do everything they can to build unity in a congregation and develop cooperation among all of God's people. Their concern for their particular congregation must not override their view of the universal church. All Christians are brothers and sisters, members of the same family, not competitors. Christian pastors are concerned for the welfare of all churches not just their own. They participate in ecumenical events and cooperative endeavors. Ecumenism is the hallmark of the Cumberland Presbyterian heritage. Schism and sectarianism are the denial of the nature of the church and can be considered to be the worst sin. They violate the spirit of Jesus Christ as expressed in his prayer in John 17.

Gossiping among members of the congregation and putting down the beliefs and practices of other churches are shameful community-breaking sins. Good pastors discourage this behavior by modeling another life style, and refusing to stoop so low.

It is possible that our approach to pastoral care creates an image of the caregiver as a sentimental, soft, pious and unoffensive person who is willing to excuse rather than deal with human sin. Some people have that image of Jesus Christ. A truer view of Jesus reveals a person with deep understanding of human nature accompanied with deep compassion; but one also who at times made a drastic approach to human problems. Jesus often confronted people with the challenge to change and take new directions in life.[26]

Examples of this are seen in the way Jesus dealt with the rich young man,[27] Nicodemus,[28] Zacchaeus,[29] Simon the Pharisee,[30] and the lawyer in the story of the Good Samaritan.[31]

FOR FURTHER CONSIDERATION

❖ Can you name the ten implications for pastoral care found in reading and studying the 23rd Psalm? Write them down and memorize them.

❖ Ezekiel identified himself with the people to whom he was to preach. How and to what extent can you as a pastor identify with the people in the church you serve, or will serve? Name the ways and discuss them.

❖ In the section about John 10:1-18 there are a number of things said describing Jesus as the good shepherd. Name them and memorize them.

❖ What do these marks of the good shepherd imply for us in our pastoral ministry? Re-read this section. Write down the implications named there. As you look at each one, ask: Do I have a potential for this trait as a pastor? How can I develop it?

---

[26] *The Rebirth of Ministry*, James D. Smart, Westminster, 1960, page 114
[27] Matthew 19:16-22
[28] John 3:1-16
[29] Luke 19:1-10
[30] Luke 7:36-50
[31] Luke 10

The effective pastor, wanting to bring people into a true relation with God, may have to confront people with the truth about themselves just as Jesus did. However, to let the confrontational style be the habitual approach is to become offensive and ineffective. One needs to understand who can be confronted with good results, and who cannot. No person or congregation wants or needs to be confronted perpetually. A good rule is to let the needs and nature of the person or congregation determine the style of approach.

There is much more which could be said about the pastoral relationship and pastoral care; however, let what has been written in this chapter suffice for the time being.

BOOKS FOR FURTHER READING

The Rebirth of Ministry, James D. Smart, Westminster, Chapter 5, "The Minister as Pastor," 1960, pp. 105-123.

Preaching and Pastoral Care, Arthur L. Teikmanis, Fortress Press, 1964, 144 pages.

Don't forget to subscribe to and read our denomination's periodicals: *The Cumberland Presbyterian* and *The Missionary Messenger.* They carry articles which are applicable to our ministry. For instance, "Ideas for Ministry—Easy Mistakes to Make," Robert Watkins, January 1990 issue. It would pay you to dig out this past issue and read this article.

The Pastor as Person, Maintaining Personal Integrity in the Choices and Challenges of Ministry, Gary L. Harbaugh, Augsburg, 1984, 172 pages. Highly recommended.

 CHAPTER 5

The Pastor as Leader of Worship

The primary function of the church is worship. Worship is central to the mission of the church. Therefore, a major role of the minister is to lead the congregation in the worship of God. In this capacity the pastor is a priest, acting as a mediator between God and the people.

> As Israel responded to God, this response pressed for expression in worship, and there was need of someone to perform the priestly office of standing as the people's representative before God, of inquiring for them concerning the will of God, then of offering their sacrifices to God and of treasuring all things that contributed to the deepening, stabilizing, and enriching of their relation to God.[1]

There is no more important charge for the pastor than that of leading in worship. It requires, first of all, a devout and sensitive spiritual life which grows in reverence and awe at the greatness and love of God. It insists that before we can lead our people, we ourselves must have entered the most holy place. If we are to call our people to prayer and praise, we must practice the Presence, and be constant learners of the art of worship.

To lead well requires special skills and resources. A casual approach is inexcusable and is an affront to the Creator. Whatever we offer to God must be our best. Sloppiness, sentimentality, folksiness and carelessness are abominations. Our leadership should always be characterized by decency, reverence, sensitivity, order and warmth of spirit.

The ordained minister is not the only one who may lead in worship. Our concept of the priesthood of believers opens the door to the laity to act as liturgists also.

> It is significant that wherever in the New Testament the term 'priesthood' is used it refers not to the special ministry but to the priestly function of the whole people of God.[2]

---

[1] *The Rebirth of Ministry*, James D. Smart, Westminster, 1960, page 53.

[2] Ibid., page 60.

The same requirements for developing skills and attitudes fall upon the lay person as well as the minister. Laypersons should not be encouraged to lead in public worship without giving them some special training. Aid should also be given laypersons who lead worship in Sunday school, Sunday school classes, CPW meetings, circle meetings, Bible study groups, and other such occasions. The benefits deriving from such efforts are reciprocal. The minister learns much from lay persons, many of whom have unique insights and skills in worship, prayer and devotion.

In addition to the tasks already mentioned here, the minister and church should provide guidance and materials for personal and family worship.

This chapter is being written on the assumption that leaders of worship must come to understand its meaning, and become acquainted with the content and forms. We will introduce the basic concepts of worship, and also include information on styles and methods of leadership.

WHAT IS WORSHIP?
AN AWARENESS OF GOD

Let us think first of worship as an experience of interaction between us and God.

Sometimes we forget, or act as if we do not know, that worship is more than ritual—more than mere acts or words.

> I am reminded of an incident at church camp. I was leader of vespers. Near the time for us to meet for the service, a little boy came to me and asked, "Is it time for gestures?" (not being adequately informed about the name and nature of the service: or was he speaking honestly?) Often in church this comes to haunt me. Gestures?[3]

As leaders of worship, we are to enable the congregation to worship God in the fullest meaning of that word. If so, how would we define worship? What is supposed to happen when we worship? What are its central elements and acts? What do we do when we worship, and what does God do?

First of all, in true worship we experience a new consciousness. We move to a different level of intensity in being, feeling and perceiving. We sense the divine Presence, the holy Other, the Utmost Reality. For some it may be a feeling of the nearness of Jesus. Or the mysterious moving of the Spirit in our midst. Jesus calls this worshipping in "spirit and in truth."[4] It is an experience above or beyond the matter-of-factness of our ordinary existence.

This can be illustrated in an experience reported by a friend. John D. attended the presentation of Handel's *Messiah* during Advent. Shortly after the opening music, he began to experience a stirring of his emotions. He was being moved out of his usual state of mind. It was more than aesthetically enjoying good music. He said he began to live *Messiah*. As he heard the old prophecies of a better day, new hope arose in him. He was awed at the announcement of Christ's coming as a

---

[3] *Soundings*, Morris Pepper, Frontier Press, 1991, page 104.

[4] John 4:20-24.

refiner's fire. He was there when the angel spoke to Mary. He was with the shepherds out in the fields when they heard the heavenly choir. He went with them to kneel at the manger. He was touched by Christ the kind shepherd who was tender with the young. The cross elicited a depressing sadness. The resurrection lifted him to the heights and his heart almost burst when he sang the Hallelujah Chorus.

His emotions had reached a fever pitch as he worshipped and was lifted to a new level of being. He said he was in a mood far beyond the power of words to express. He was so energized that it took several hours for his feelings to subside. The experience made a big difference in his life.

This kind of event is not a part of every service we attend. Many times we just go through the motions. In spite of this, however, we can always pray and hope that God will break through into our lives and lift us out of our ordinariness.

The Book of Psalms provides some other examples of true worship. The Psalms were written out of the experiences of David and other persons. They move on a level of worship and are expressions of the heart to God. They were used as a means of worship by the Hebrews in making confession, giving praise and adoration, affirming faith, crying to God out of deep distress and in consecrating themselves. Some of these Psalms become both a means of being brought into a relation with God and expressing worship of God. This is the reason we use many of them in our services today. Even a private reading of them silently or aloud can become worship of the highest quality. It may be beneficial to stop now and read one devotionally.[5]

This brings us to our first definition of worship. Perhaps what we have already said will have informed the definitions we give.

FIRST DEFINITION

> Christian worship is the deliberate act of seeking to approach reality at its deepest level by becoming aware of God in and through Jesus Christ and by responding to this awareness.[6]

The author of the above definition says further:

> Worship involves a shift in gears as far as our normal consciousness is concerned. Much of life is like listening to a scratched record in which we constantly hear the record noise but only at intervals become aware of the beautiful music being played beneath the din.[7]

We are to make a deliberate effort to approach reality. This is part of our responsibility in worship. We do not come first to be acted upon. We come to church with an intention to be a part of the action ourselves. We come seeking. So we prepare ourselves by prayer and expectancy, and by sharpening our attention.

---

[5] Select from Psalms 8, 103, 104, 111, 113, 122, 139.

[6] *New Forms of Worship*, James F. White, Abingdon, 1971, page 40.

[7] Ibid., page 40.

However, we could do all in our power to find God and fail miserably, unless God were seeking us too. This is the double search in worship. God seeking us and our seeking God.

Although we are to "seek God while he may be found," we cannot manipulate God into coming. It is up to God. We believe, however, that God wills to come to us, and so we seek in faith. God is the initiator of the encounter, and quickens our hearts.

> In worship God claims persons in Christ and offers assurance of love, forgiveness, and guidance and redemption.[8]

The awareness of God elicits a response, often spontaneously, when we realize all that God does for us. One of the high points of worship is an outburst of praise and thanksgiving like that found in the 103rd Psalm.

Other responses include confession of sin, receiving forgiveness, praying that our needs and the needs of our neighbors will be filled, offering ourselves for mission, and going out into the world with the intention of making a difference. We will say more about our responses in worship later.

THE MAIN POINT

The main point we have been trying to make is that to worship is, first of all, to be made aware of God. Otherwise there is only motion, word, and emptiness. But with it there is Presence and Power. It is essential that we pastors realize that our purpose is to lead the people into such an awareness. We want to relate them to the ultimate source of their being. This is our priestly charge. In so doing we move from the center of the stage.

> The relationship of a pastor to individuals, groups, and congregations undergoes a metamorphosis in the act of worship. Consciousness of his presence fades out and awareness of the real presence of God reaches its zenith.[9]

A SECOND DEFINITION

Worship, as Gaines S. Dobbins has said, is the "interruption of our routine" and of our involvement in the transitory things of life "to recognize the supreme worth of God, to praise him for his goodness, to meditate on his holiness, to renew devotion to his service" and to sever our idolatries.[10]

This definition points to an absolute necessity if we are to find reality. We have to get out of our routine which is so much a part of us that it is almost like shedding our skin. We have to break the hold of the transitory. We have to sever our idolatries. This is strong medicine, but urgent. We are enslaved to the temporal, and we have to break the chains if we are to find what is real. This suggests that there is a self-discipline we have to exercise if we are to grow spiritually. We have

---

[8] *Confession of Faith*, 1984, 5.13, page 13.

[9] *The Christian Pastor*, Wayne Oates, Westminster, 1964, page 120.

[10] Ibid., Pages 120, 121.

to affirm that God only is supreme and all else is finite. We are speaking here of a radical modification if our worship is not to be a sham.

The world impinges upon us. It even invades the sacred hours in the sanctuary.

> I was leading vespers at Ovoca near Tullahoma, Tennessee. It became noisy. The main gate of the grounds had been left open accidently. Cars drove by in numbers. Roosters crowed. Dogs barked. Children cried and cried. One after another and then in chorus. It became so ridiculous, we stopped and laughed. What else? These disturbances were facts and symbols of our existence: noise, movement, unhappiness, and human need. We live and worship right in the midst of pandemonium.[11]

We cannot get completely away from the world. Nor do we want to. We work out our faith and make our witness here. But unless we break away from it and deny its hold on us, at least for a little while, we cannot enter the other world.

A THIRD DEFINITION

We are impressed with the definition given by Harold M. Daniels. It emphasizes some things we have been saying, and opens our thoughts to others. We will make no comment on it, but let it stand by itself.

> Christian worship is an *encounter* with life at its deepest level of meaning; a *celebration* of God as a dynamic, active, energizing presence at the heart of life; an *affirmation* that life has ultimate meaning, for in Jesus we discover what it means to be fully human; a *response* to live a resurrection life of newness and future possibilities, of growth and becoming, to take part in building a new world—a world of justice, peace and love.[12]

A FOURTH DEFINITION

Let us now consider worship as celebration.

> Christian worship is the affirmation of God's living presence and the celebration of God's mighty acts.[13]

It has been said "to celebrate is to make an event with joy." Joy is a mark of our faith. The angels announced to the shepherds "good news of great joy." Jesus said he came "that our joy might be full." The Psalmist wrote of the "joy of salvation." Paul called on us to "rejoice always."

Other elements in celebration are remembrance, thanksgiving and praise, and dedication or rededication. Worship as celebration then, may be defined as follows:

---

[11] *Soundings*, Morris Pepper, Frontier, 1991, page 117.
[12] *What to Do with Sunday Morning*, Harold M. Daniels, Westminster, 1979, pages 20, 21.
[13] *Confession of Faith*, Frontier, 1984, page 13.

> Worship as celebration is to remember the mighty acts of God, to respond in joyful thanksgiving and praise, and to dedicate or rededicate ourselves to God.

There are other connotations for worship as celebration. They are expressed well in these words:

> Christian worship is always celebration. This is so because a victory is the basis of Christian worship. It is the victory of Almighty God through Jesus Christ. It is God's victory over our death and for our life; it is the triumph of his purpose to redeem his whole creation to willing responsiveness to him. It is victory that was won in principle by the death and resurrection of Jesus Christ, and now is to be realized in full. Because it is victory, the whole telling forth (announcing, proclaiming of what God has done, will do, and is doing through Jesus Christ is called the gospel—"good news.") It is "good news" that calls for thankful rejoicing in a different way from any other good news, for God's victory through Jesus Christ is the single source of meaning and hope for our lives. Christian worship, then, however solemn or exuberant, however simple or elaborate, has its meaning in the victorious love if God.[14]

The concept of worship as celebration is a corrective of the approach which we often make. It is upbeat with qualities of exuberance and exultation in contrast to the dullness, casualness, joylessness and unexpectancy of some worship. The idea of victory and celebration gives a lilt to our church going.

CORPORATE WORSHIP AS DIALOGUE

The two following quotes point out that worship is a dialogue and that it is corporate.

> The Directory stresses the initiative of God in worship: it is God who speaks, and it is God who calls forth the response of his people. In worship, God speaks through scripture and sermon, and through the Sacraments, bearing witness to himself; and in worship, God's Holy Spirit urges our grateful response through prayers and praise, in offering, and in our communion with him. Therefore, Christian worship does have the character of a conversation, of hearing and speaking, of seeing and acting, of a good, glad dialogue with God through the Spirit. In this dialogue, all the people are involved and not simply minister and choir.
>
> The Service of the Lord's Day is an act of corporate worship. It is not something in which solitary souls sit together as spectators at a drama or lecture. Instead, Christian worship is the grateful, united response of a people who are called by the Lord and who participate as one body in his service.[15]

THE LORD'S DAY

Further, our *Confession of Faith* points out that although we can worship God at any time and place, there has been set aside one special day for corporate or

---

[14] *The Celebration of the Gospel*, Hardin, Quillian, White, Abingdon, 1964, pages 13, 14.

[15] *The Book of Common Worship*, Provisional Services, Westminster, 1966, pages 139, 140.

public worship. It is the Lord's Day. It is the first day of the week, the day on which Christ rose from the dead, and is appointed for Christians to worship in remembrance of the resurrection of Jesus. Hence, we understand each Sunday to be an Easter day, celebrating the resurrection of our Lord.

Also, the Lord's Day commemorates the first day of creation. We worship on that day remembering God's creation of the universe and declaring that it is good.[16]

A MODEL WORSHIP EXPERIENCE

We need models to personify concepts and meanings for us, thus making them more realistic and understandable. A model encounter with God would make more vivid our perceptions of worship, while also providing us a guide for planning and directing.

A classical model is found in Isaiah 6. We call it classical because it is central to genuine worship; that is, it holds the essential elements of worship and depicts what happens in an interaction between God and persons. It is an example of both inward response and outward form, of content and structure. It exemplifies the process of experiential worship as it moves from stage to stage becoming embodied in a specific framework. Although it is a dynamic transaction, it takes an identifiable form as it unfolds.

Let us now read Isaiah 6:1-8, and get clearly into our minds the details of the event. We will then mark each stage of the happening as it progresses, and note the various elements in it.

As we do this let us remember we are thinking of corporate worship, worship as a body of believers, and not private devotions. Isaiah went to the temple with a company of believers. We are not told how they responded to God's call. Each person, though related to others in the temple, was free to make her or his own answer. We are social creatures and need each other. Private worship is not enough. We find God more fully in company with others, individually making our own response, yet sharing in each other's experiences, and contributing mutually to everyone. Although Isaiah had to answer for himself, he doubtless experienced God in a way he would not have in private. That is true of all of us.

WHY WORSHIP?

First of all, we need to ask a fundamental question. Why did Isaiah go to the temple to worship?

It has been suggested that he went from *a sense of need* arising out of the death of King Uzziah. Verse 1a. "In the year that King Uzziah died." (RSV) This is more than the marking of a date; it signals a crisis of loss. The king is dead. One interpretation is that Isaiah, Israel's young prophet, had hoped that through Uzziah's support many things would be accomplished for good in the kingdom. Now Uzziah is gone and Isaiah's hopes are crushed. A Jewish tradition indicates that Isaiah might have been a cousin of Uzziah. If so, his grief and discouragement would be intensified because of the death of a member of the family.

This caused him to turn to the only source of strength and courage which was

---

[16] *Confession of Faith*, Directory for Worship, Frontier, 1984, pages 80, 81.

left. No longer could he depend upon help from a human being. He must turn to God. So out of his need he went to the temple.

We also worship out of a sense of need. A sense of need may grow out of matters such as an unsolved problem, the lack of moral strength, sorrow, loss, a longing to express thanks, moral and spiritual failure, sin, a longing for companionship, and the need for guidance. "We are not sufficient unto ourselves and we experience a sense of completeness and fulfillment through the encounter with and worship of our Creator."[17]

A sense of need makes us more receptive to God's help and moves us to seek the presence of One who can sustain and comfort. Our inadequacy is apparent every day. Our need for God rests heavily on us. This is not, however, the whole truth about our motivation toward worship.

Why do we worship? Dr. Turner Clinard provides some answers in these words:

> Worship is response to the loving action of God. Worship begins in remembering what God has done for us, and continues in the expression of thanksgiving for God's redemptive love... One worships because of his [or her] vital relationship with God and in order to keep that relationship vital... One worships, not because he is good or thinks he is, but because he knows he is not as good as he ought to be.[18]

Dr. Clinard further points out on the negative side that we do not worship to get something. Nor do we go to church "to get something out of it." We worship God because we have already gotten something, and we want to praise and thank God for it.

Our *Confession of Faith*, in the initial paragraphs in the Directory for Worship, seems to say we worship because God invites us and seeks a relationship with us. Jesus said, "...True worshippers will worship the Father in spirit and truth, for such the Father *seeks* to worship him."[19]

Everything in the gospel points to the fact that God seeks us like the shepherd looking for lost sheep. We can say, then, that we worship *in response* to God's reaching out to us. "Deep calleth unto deep..."[20] The deep in God calls to the deep in us. It is interesting that these words are written in the same Psalm in which the writer is expressing his longing for God. "As the hart longs for flowing streams so longs my soul for thee, O God."[21] It is all tied together for those who belong to God, even for those who have not responded. We long for and reach out toward God and God longs for and reaches out to us, and there is meeting, communion, celebration and joy beyond containment.

Some of the most poignant words about God's seeking us, even those who constantly reject him, are these:

---

[17] *Confession of Faith*, Directory for Worship, Frontier, 1984, page 80.

[18] *Becoming A Christian*, Turner N. Clinard, Tidings, 1976, page 51.

[19] John 4:23.

[20] Psalms 42:7.

[21] Psalms 42:1.

> I was ready to be sought by those who did not ask for me;
> I was ready to be found by those who did not seek me.
> I said, "Here am I, here am I." to a nation that did not call my name.
> I spread out my hands all the day to a rebellious people,
> who walk in a way that is not good,
> following their own devices...
> who say, "Keep to yourself, do not come near me, for I am set apart from you."[22]

> When Israel was a child, I loved him, and out of Egypt I called my son.
> The more I called them, the more they went from me;
> They kept sacrificing to the Baals, and burning incense to idols.
> Yet is was I who taught Ephraim to walk, I took them up in my arms;
> But they did not know that I healed them.
> I led them with cords of compassion, with bands of love,
> And I became to them as one who eases the yoke on their jaws,
> and I bent down to them and fed them...
>
> How can I give you up, O Ephraim! How can I hand you over, O Israel!
> How can I make you like Admah! How can I treat you like Zeboiim!
> My heart recoils within me, my compassion grows warm and tender.[23]

Read also Isaiah 55:1-9. Why do we worship? Because we are in need. Because of what God has done for us. Because God seeks us and finds us. And probably for many other reasons we do not know or understand. It is a mystery!

REALIZATION OF GOD'S PRESENCE

"In the year that King Uzziah died I saw the Lord sitting upon a throne, high and lifted up; and his train filled the temple." (Verse 1 RSV) Isaiah had an unusual vision of God and felt God's presence intensely.

> The conjectured circumstances of the vision itself are these: At some great religious festival held during the year that King Uzziah died Isaiah was present in his official capacity as a prophet. Standing with the priests between the porch and the altar, he watched the play and movement of the ancient ceremony, so rich in symbolism, in color and in music. To the worshipers it was a drama, familiar but still enthralling, that and nothing more. But to Isaiah, who had walked with God and grown ever more sensitive to spiritual and eternal values, suddenly there came an awareness of the divine reality behind the symbolism. The vision is described in terms of the ceremony, but the interpretation Isaiah put upon things visible is proof of his spiritual perception... In that supreme moment Isaiah stood alone with God. The earthly scene faded, the sound of singing died away, and he saw the Lord sitting upon a throne.[24]

---

[22] Isaiah 65:1-2, 5.

[23] Hosea 11:4, 9.

[24] *The Interpreter's Bible*, Volume 5, Isaiah, Abingdon Press, 1956, page 205.

The vision Isaiah had was of a kingly presence ("sitting upon a throne"), and a holy presence ("High and lifted up"). The whole temple was filled with God. ("His train filled the temple.") Isaiah was not only surrounded but was immersed in God. To all others the occasion may have been ceremony, pomp and circumstance; but to Isaiah it was Divine Presence (Shekinah) and meeting. He was captivated with awe and wonder.[25]

Isaiah's worship probably appears so intense in contrast to ours on any given Sunday that there seems to be no similarity between the two. This should not be reason for our being discouraged. We are created for a relationship with our Creator. Each of us can come to know and experience God.

It is essential that we expect and anticipate, be open to, and pray for, an opening to the loving Father as we come to church. It is also incumbent upon leaders to provide the most effective means possible of helping people become aware of the Lord's presence.

The instrumental prelude, the call to worship, and a worshipful environment are used to help set the mood for devotion. They often seem to be inadequate in view of the great experience which could await our people in the sanctuary. We need to find additional and new ways and means for this purpose.

More needs to be said from the New Testament viewpoint about God's presence in worship. We Christians are able to think of the presence and coming of the Lord in terms of the Holy Spirit. The Holy Spirit is a dynamic, active, energizing Person who brings about changes; who acts with power; who comes and goes at will; and who cannot be manipulated for our purposes and whims.

It is not proper or right to speak of our *having* the Holy Spirit, though some do. Rather, scripturally, we must speak and think of the Holy Spirit as having, owning, possessing and directing *us*. The Holy Spirit is in charge; not we.

Therefore, when we think of encountering our Maker, one aspect of worship is not actively seeking but inactively waiting in patience, humility, and hope for the Lord to come; knowing that God does not await our coming; but we await God's. "I wait for the Lord, my soul waits, and in his word I hope; my soul waits for the Lord more than watchmen for the morning, more than watchmen for the morning."[26]

The Lord we wait for is the Holy Spirit, who makes real the facts of our redemption and enables us to internalize them; who comes with fire and flame;[27] who gives aid, comfort and strength;[28] who confronts, convinces and leads to the truth.[29]

If this is the kind of Presence we meet in the assembly, then more is needed than being still in order to know (though that is essential). It is being willing to

---

[25] "The Hebrew root for dwell is sh-k-n, from which the post-biblical word *Shekinah* is derived. The use of the term naturally carries with it the idea of God's presence." *A Theological Word Book of the Bible*, Richardson, Macmillan, 1950, page 176.

[26] Psalms 130:5, 6.

[27] Acts 2.

[28] John 14:15.

[29] John 16:8-15.

surrender and to obey. This approach is rooted in reality about ourselves; we are independent and rebellious and we need to repent and submit.

But back to Isaiah in the temple. From what finally happened in his experience, he had evidently come with a willingness to follow God's leadership. This opened the door to God.

PRAISE AND ADORATION OF GOD

"Above him stood the seraphim; each one had six wings; with two he covered his face, and with two he covered his feet, and with two he flew. And one called to another and said:

> 'Holy, holy, holy is the Lord of hosts;
> the whole earth is full of his glory!'

And the foundations of the thresholds shook at the voice of him who called, and the house was filled with smoke." (Verses 2, 3, 4 RSV)

The recognition of God's presence and nature brought forth praise and adoration from Isaiah and the angelic host. They sang, "holy, holy, holy." The word *holy* means absolute perfection, purity and goodness. The holy God is separate from all creation, and above all. The Almighty is transcendent, wholly apart in nature and being.

It is natural for us to burst forth into praise and adoration when we recognize and behold God's true nature as Creator, Ruler and Redeemer. The seraphim and Isaiah did it in song. David did it in the marvellous words of Psalm 8 out of the realization of the majesty and power of Jehovah. (This Psalm should be read today in the light of our new knowledge of space. It will add infinitesimal dimensions to our concept of the Creator and Maintainer of the universe.)

Part of the wonder and awe evinced from Isaiah evidently was educed by the comprehension that this separate, holy, transcendent Being, who was apart from all existence, had elected to visit those in the temple. The transcendent had become immanent (present thorugh all things), filling the house with divine glory. That too, is a part of our own adoration, originating out of awe and wonder that the Mighty Creator came, and comes, and shares intimately with us through Jesus Christ and the Holy Spirit.

As we remember on the Lord's Day, and in other times of our corporate worship, how God has shown love to us in Jesus Christ, our hearts are touched with the cost of our salvation, and made to give praise for mercy and grace.

The Sacrament of the Lord's Supper, central to our Christian worship, is one of the means to this end. As we lift the bread and the cup to our lips in remembrance of Christ's self-giving love, praise pours forth from our lips and humbled hearts.

> The dominant character of Christian worship is praise of God. Because of who God is, what God has done, and what God has promised to do, it is in order for us to praise God for that steadfast love which is peculiar to God.[30]

---

[30] *The Confession of Faith*, Directory for Worship, Frontier, 1984, page 80.

> Praise is based upon the prior love of God. "We love because he loved us first." We praise him because his love has again been disclosed to us in worship. Praise is the basic and inevitable response to rediscovery of the activity of God, to the fresh awareness "from whom all blessings flow."[31]

A word of caution. We need to remember that Isaiah's experience was extremely dramatic, and not typical in its imagery, and manifestation, but only in its content. In speaking of worship, and in planning for it, let's keep in mind that many, or perhaps most, people have a quiet, undramatic sense of God affirmed by faith, if not by feeling and imagination, when they worship; but nevertheless real. Although drama has its value in worship, we need not aim at it so much as at reality.

An aside. If some of our statements about the presence, the coming and going, the seeking and withholding of God seem to be contradictory, just remember that our faith is paradoxical and does not always fit into our neatly reasoned out theology. It is a part of the mystery.

PENITENCE AND CONFESSION OF SIN

"And I said, Woe is me! for I am lost; for I am a man of unclean lips, and I dwell in the midst of a people of unclean lips; for my eyes have seen the King, the Lord of hosts!" (Verse 5 RSV) The KJ version uses *undone* instead of the RSV *lost*. *Lost* is a relational term. It denotes that one is out of right relationships and does not know where one is. The word *undone* seems to connote that Isaiah feels he is coming apart, going to pieces, out of control, disintegrated and baffled; all of which are fitting descriptions of a person who is out of relationship with God, oneself and others. The word *unclean* suggests that isaiah feels unworthy of being in the temple and in the presence of a holy being.

Isaiah had seen a God of holiness and purity, of majesty and power and in contrast he saw himself as being impure and unholy. He confessed not only for himself but for the people of whom he was a part. It is possible that the young ambitious prophet Isaiah might have thought going to the temple would open a way for God to give him strength to go out into the world to clean up the mess there, engaging in a moral reformation and straightening out the sinners in the Kingdom. If so, he was sidetracked from this purpose. He found that he must begin with himself. *He* was the one who needed to be reformed; and so in humility and need he made his confession.

This provides a model and a hope for our own worship. Once we are made conscious of God, we become deeply aware of our own unworthiness and guilt. If a part of our worship is remembering, as we have already agreed, then to remember and to be made aware of Christ and his life, death and resurrection is to elicit not only praise but penitence and confession; for measured against Jesus Christ, we are utter failures. The promise of the gospel is that if we repent we will be forgiven. Opportunities for repentance and confession are included in every service of true worship. Since we are sinners saved by grace, and not by works, we need to make regular confession to each other and to the Lord.

---

[31] *New forms of Worship*, James F. White, Abingdon, 1971, page 42.

SENSE OF FORGIVENESS

"Then flew one of the seraphim to me, having in his hand a burning coal which he had taken with tongs from the altar. And he touched my mouth, and said: Behold, this has touched your lips; your guilt is taken away, and your sin is forgiven." (Verse 6 RSV)

Evidently, somewhere from his Hebrew faith Isaiah had become acquainted with the idea of God's forgiveness to those who confess. For no sooner than he had cried out his feeling of woe because of his sin, he knew God forgave and cleansed him of sin. This can become true for any who come to worship with a burden of sin if they make their confession in faith. This is the central part of the gospel we celebrate in worship.

There are those in every gathering for worship who bring a sense of guilt and who need pardon. An opportunity, then, should be given in every service for confession and forgiveness on the part of individuals and the congregation as a whole.

Some churches use silent, and/or unison prayers of confession for this purpose, which are followed by a declaration of pardon and words of assurance of forgiveness. Some churches do not follow this practice; but in whatever way this may be planned for, it is an essential part of worship.

An appropriate hymn following the declaration of pardon would be one of thanksgiving and praise for the salvation which is ours in Jesus Christ.

THE CALL OF GOD

Immediately following Isaiah's cleansing from sin the Word of God came with urgency and clarity concerning something which should be done. There is a definite relation between our worship and the needs in the world. Many seem to feel that the experience of salvation and worship is complete when they have accepted the forgiveness of God. They assume they are free to go on their way rejoicing in their blessings. Isaiah himself might have supposed this to be true and was surprised that God issued a new summons to him. However; "Whom shall I send and who will go for us" is the challenge Isaiah heard. (Verse 8a RSV)

It is interesting that the call of God seemed to be general—to everyone. "*Who will go for us?*" Isaiah was moved to respond for himself. Is this not still true? God calls everyone to service, and gives grace to those who are ready to say yes.

No true worship experience is complete until we have heard that call; for we cannot worship God in spirit and in truth without being conscious, under God's leadership, of some need or needs which are all around us, and about which we must do something.

The call of God gave in the temple indicates that in every worship, at the proper time, God's Word comes to us. It may come at any time to anyone or all, for God is free to act at will. God's call seemed to have come to Isaiah directly without any human instrument, although there were priests presiding over the event and they might have spoken the Word. Either can be true today. Regardless, in the development of worship over the years, we have accepted the reading and preaching of the Word as traditionally a major way through which God speaks to us. We believe the Almighty speaks to us through the Word which is contained in the Bible, and can do so also through a message prepared by the minister. We do not believe these to be the only way we receive the divine message.

THE RESPONSE OF DEDICATION

When God calls we either react or respond. Isaiah's response was "Here I am! Send me." (Verse 8b RSV) No worship experience is complete until we have made our response to God and have consecrated ourselves to the purpose, life, work or task to which we have been summoned. Through a voluntary act of the will, we answer. The Lord cannot answer for us; nor will the Lord force us to do so. It is up to us to surrender and commit ourselves.

That to which Isaiah dedicated himself was both immediate and continual. He asked, "Lord, how long?" The answer in paraphrase was "Until your task is completed." (Verse 11.) Our worship finds fulfillment in a life of continual surrender as we live it out in the world.

We are attempting to relate Isaiah's experience in the temple to our worship today, using it as a model or guide. In planning worship accordingly, this particular stage of dedication is a time in which we give opportunity for the people to respond to the Word in commitment. They may do so by answering the invitation to Christian Discipleship, committing themselves to a specific life work, rededicating themselves, making an offering, and in other appropriate ways.

SOME IMPLICATIONS

Before we go further, there are some things to be noted about using this model for worship.

First, all the above elements are essential for a complete worship experience, and are a biblically authoritative and reliable guide in planning services. Ordinarily, all the elements can be used for any given worship liturgy.

Second, although Isaiah's experience seemed to move or flow naturally from one stage to another, it is not to be expected that if we plan by the model that the people's experience will move accordingly. We are all different and are at different stages of growth and need. So, regardless of our plans, people are free to respond at will. However, this does not excuse us from planning. The Isaiah model is a good one to follow. We are not bound by it, and are free to make variations of it from time to time, giving emphasis to certain elements at different times, such as having a Praise Service with emphasis on praise; of giving emphasis in a service to confession and forgiveness; or holding prayer services with emphasis on prayers of different kinds.

The above model does not include some elements and means customarily used in a service; such as prayer, an offering, hymns, etc. However, it lends itself to the inclusion of these in proper order.

THE ORDINARY ACTS OF WORSHIP

From this model, from tradition and from the *Confession of Faith*, Directory for Worship, we can say that the ordinary acts of worship are these:

Praise of God
Confession of Sin

Proclamation
Affirmation of Faith
Offering
Commitment and Commissioning
Celebration of the Sacraments

OTHER OCCASIONS OF WORSHIP

The Directory for Worship gives resources for the celebration of Baptism and the Lord's Supper; and also for the wedding, the funeral, individual and family worship. It is suggested that a reading of the entire Directory for Worship at this particular time would be beneficial and informative.

It should be understood that the Cumberland Presbyterian denomination has never had an official liturgy prescribed for use in its congregations. We have what is called free worship. That is, we can plan and use a variety of resources for our services. However, the above discussion points to a model which would guide us into the use of forms, ideas and resources which are essential to true worship based upon the Bible and the traditions of our heritage. We will do well to follow it rather than to act as freelancers in this area so important to the spiritual life of our people.

We are now ready to enter into the consideration of some practical matters having to do with the conduct of public worship. Time and space forbid our going into great detail concerning these matters. This can wait until another stage of learning is reached in preparation for ministry when a fuller study of this subject can be made. The following ideas have been garnered from many sources, most of which cannot be acknowledged for their source was not recorded. It is hoped that this might be acceptable and not become a cause for incarceration for plagiarism.

SOME RESPONSIBILITIES OF THE PASTOR IN WORSHIP

As a rule, *the pastor is responsible* for planning the worship for the congregation. Decisions on the form of the liturgy, the materials to be used, and the elements to be included belong to the pastor. The music personnel should be consulted. In many churches the pastors work with their worship committees.

Early planning will facilitate the process of preparing for worship on the part of the choir, and others who participate in the services, and will allow time for the printing of bulletins and other materials which need to be used. Some situations call for a modification of this rule; however, the church session, under the leadership of the pastor, has the final word and is the final authority in making decisions about the worship of the church.

We cannot over-emphasize *the benefits of relying on the Directory of Worship* in the *Confession of Faith* as a resource and guide for planning and directing worship. This is the officially recommended guide in the Cumberland Presbyterian Church and has been written by qualified persons. It provides alternative orders of worship and a diversity of resources adaptable to varying situations and needs.

Further, there is *a fruitful production of additional aids* from many sources for the enrichment of services. Our denomination has been a partner with the Presbyterian Church U.S.A. in the publication of such materials as: *The Service for the Lord's Day, Holy Baptism and Services for the Renewal of Baptism, Christian Marriage,* and *The Funeral,* A Service of Witness to the Resurrection. These are available through our Book Store. Materials from these sources can be adapted to different congregations.

Worship materials (hymns, liturgies, responses, etc.) which enable people to respond with meaning and joy *on their own cultural level* should be selected. Pastors are to enable the people to worship in spirit and truth and so they plan accordingly. If there is a divergency between the level on which the pastor worships and that on which the people worship, preference must be given to the people. This does not mean, however, that the pastor is not responsible for trying to aim at a higher quality of worship. Nor does it mean the pastor should not adapt to the situation and try to learn to worship on another level and to understand how and why the people respond as they do. If pastors expect the people to change, why should they not be willing to change also? There should be no double standard here.

It is wise to remember, however, that *we do not change easily in this regard.* It is difficult to develop appreciation for the new and to change old mores and customs. Many a pastor has fallen upon unhappy circumstances because of ignoring and failing to appreciate and respect the culture of other persons. As priests, our first duty is to bring them into a relationship with God through means that can elicit the best response. We will be wise to seek out first the "track" or "wave length" which they are on and not try to find new and unbeaten channels too quickly. Learning to wait with patience and to give people time before making too many changes is a lesson most of us need.

Having said this, now let us say that *pastors are responsible for teaching the meaning of worship and introducing new materials and hymns.* This can be done in formal and in informal ways. Since we believe in the educational process, and that people can change, we are bound to assume the role of educator in this field. Can we not believe also that if people get a better understanding of the subject and what is expected of them when they come to church, they will respond to newer and better ways?

It may lead to improvement for pastors to *take a good look at the place of worship.* Is it conducive to a mood of devotion? Does it have an atmosphere of warmth? Are the lights properly located? Too bright or too dim? Would symbols and banners enhance and enrich the service? How about the seating? Are the seats comfortable? Do they provide visible access to everyone?

A word of caution about seating. We are all aware of the practice of the congregation with regard to sitting on the back seats, and leaving a lot of empty timber near the front. We are also aware that people like to sit where they sit, and usually do not want to be moved. God seems to come to them better in their own pew.

How we would like to change some of this! If any changes are to be considered let them be discussed with the flock first. If so, they'll probably opt for things to remain as they are; but they might have become a little more aware of some better possibilities. If we are careful, we may win some and get them on our side. Let's not get our hopes too high, too soon, though. Neither should we think our ideas are always the best. Some of the people have been there a long time and their ideas must be respected.

Another bother. *How do we handle the way people gather for worship?* Should we encourage them to talk and visit before the service begins? Or should we try to teach them to come in reverently and quietly in preparation for worship?

One opinion is that they ought to be allowed to talk and visit; that they are thus becoming a group; and are establishing communication among themselves. But, how ready are they to be aware of God, if they do this? Can they switch moods rapidly from gossip to adoration? From chit-chat to prayer? From football to confession? From idle talk to service? (And, what about those men who stand outside and come in only when the first hymn begins?)

We should encourage the people to spend some time in quietness in order to make a break between the world outside and the sanctuary inside; to put out of their minds the secular confusions of their lives, and turn their thoughts toward the gospel. Can we really expect this of any congregation today? Can we shift from earth to heaven that quickly? Or from *things* to *Spirit*? Or from the secular to the holy? Some think so; some think not.

If we decide to request people to be quiet as they enter the church, then it is important for everyone to comply, lest the saints who are trying to meditate lose their devotional spirits from anger at those who are still talking!

Is this the kind of problem we can solve? Maybe so. Maybe not. But we need to work on it.

The word *liturgy* comes from the Greek word *Leitourgia*, which is derived from *Leos* (people) and *Ergon* (work). It means the work of the people. If the service is to be the work of the people, then they ought to be given every possible opportunity to take part in it. It must not become the work of the leader only. In view of what has already been said about the priesthood of all believers, we must engage the laity in acts of worship to the extent that it is possible. They should be encouraged to take part in the singing, the responses, the litanies, the prayers, the offerings, as well as to listen. Let this be a guiding principle for us. It will yield fruit in the spiritual development of the people and the enrichment of our services.

SOME HINTS ON LEADING IN WORSHIP

1. *Enable the people to worship.* Omit anything that might be a hindrance to this end. Do all you can to facilitate the people's response.

2. *Leading in worship is an art.* "Art—The creation or the expression of what is beautiful...something in which imagination and personal taste are more important than exact measurement and calculation."[32]

> It should be clear, therefore, that public worship is closer to the fine arts than to the practical... Here the subject matter is the truth concerning the ways of God in his dealings with [humankind], supremely in Christ; the appeal is to the souls of the persons whom he is calling to become children, as well as his agents in advancing his kingdom... Except in the realm of religious poetry... where is the artist who uses words and melodies for such heavenly purposes as we ministers use them whenever we lead in the public worship of God?... So let us think about the meaning of public worship as a fine art, and then about the leader as an artist second to none among men.[33]

---

[32] *Oxford Student's Dictionary of American English*, A.S. Hornby, Oxford, 1983, page 32.
[33] *The Fine Art of Public Worship*, Andrew W. Blackwood, Abingdon, 1939, page 14.

An art is something we must learn, and to learn we must practice it. We must also learn all we can about it. To accept this concept is to do all we can to become skilled in this most important art. It will save us from lazy, sloppy, coarse, crude and insensitive attitudes and acts. On the other hand, it will create within us those attitudes of humility and reverence which befit those who are to minister in the sanctuary.

3. *Do and say only what is necessary for the people to know how to participate and no more.* Triteness and wordiness are sins against good communication; are boring; and may interfere with the mood of devotion.

4. *Don't put on an air of superficial piety.* A holy tone in the voice and an assumed attitude of religiosity are anathema in a place where reality is being sought. Equally out of place is a lighthearted approach as if one is leading cheers at a pep rally. Neither is there a place for gloom and doom, and a sad-faced demeanor; we are celebrating the resurrection.

5. *Lead in worship by worshipping.* Our attitude of devotion will communicate itself to others. We join in worship with the people and thus lead them by our own participation. We are not merely announcing the items on a program.

We leaders of worship have a double duty. It demands a great deal from us, but we must pay the price if we are to minister well. We not only worship with the congregation; but we are responsible for seeing that the service moves at the proper pace, that it does not go overtime, that nothing will distract from the service if we can prevent it; and to do all we can to make it acceptable to God and beneficial to the people.

6. *Avoid acts, comments, and dress which might distract or call attention to ourselves.* The less members of the congregation are aware of the preacher, and the more they are aware of the Presence, the more they are enabled to worship. A clerical robe, designed to represent the office and downplay show, or conservative clothing are recommended. The present trend toward more color in robes and stoles may add tone, but also may divert attention to the wrong person. We are not doing theatrics; we are doing devotion.

7. *Be direct and forceful.*[34] Speak loudly enough for everyone to hear, including those with hearing problems and devices. Leave no uncertainty in giving directions. No one benefits by mumbling from the lectern or pulpit.

8. *Plan carefully all comments and leadership directions.*[35] Be careful of spontaneous remarks, or off-the-cuff directions. We should go over the entire service before the hour and plan each step well.

9. *Learn how to lead non-verbally.*[36] The less said by the leader in moving from one element of worship to another the better. We do not always have to tell the people when to be seated; we can indicate it by motion of hand or a nod of the head. If the people are familiar with the service, they probably know when to stand and sit.

10. *Lead behind or in front of the pulpit?* Some ministers move around considerably in their leading worship and in preaching. Too much movement is

---

[34] *The Confession of Faith,* 1984, Directory for Worship, page 95.

[35] Ibid., pages 95, 96.

[36] Ibid., page 96.

distracting. We may move from the pulpit and nearer the people in making initial announcements at the beginning of the service. In most cases, leading from behind or beside the pulpit, or from the lectern is recommended.

11. *Enable the service to flow integrally and coherently.* Avoid injecting greetings, notices, forgotten announcements into the process of worship. It is rude to interrupt our conversation with God. Nothing should disrupt the flow from praise, to confession, to assurance, to hearing the Word, to affirmation, to commitment.

CONCLUSION

This chapter has been introductory, and does not claim to include all we need to know about worship. It is a starter largely for beginners in ministry. Perhaps its best value will be to stimulate the reader to further learning.

FOR FURTHER READING AND STUDY

The Service for the Lord's Day, Supplemental Liturgical Resource 1, Prepared by the Joint Office of Worship for the Presbyterian Church (U.S.A.) and the Cumberland Presbyterian Church, Published by the Westminster Press, 1984, 192 pages.

Other Supplemental Liturgical Resources (SLR) include the following:

Holy Baptism and Services for the Renewal of Baptism, SLR 2.

Christian Marriage, SLR 3.

The Funeral, A Service of Witness to the Resurrection, SLR 4.

Confession of Faith, 1984, Directory for Worship, Frontier Press, pages 80-110.

Preaching and Leading in Worship, William H. Willimon, Westminster Press, 1984, 111 pages.

FOR FURTHER CONSIDERATION

- With reference to the terms "leader in worship" and "liturgist," which do you prefer? To what extent have you worshipped according to the thoughts on pages 72-74?

- Do you accept the definitions of worship in this chapter? Do the definitions indicate more expectations in worship than can ordinarily be experienced?

- How can we teach congregations the meaning of worship? How can we aid the parishioners in preparing for worship? What more can we do than we are now doing to enable people to worship on deeper levels?

- To what extent is the model in Isaiah 6 a help to you in planning worship?

- Why do you think the people of your church come to worship? Are you willing to accept the responsibilities in leading worship as suggested in this chapter? In your situation, what changes need to be made in improving worship, and how would you go about making them?

 CHAPTER 6

The Pastor As Preacher

THAT SERMON!

We preachers live under the pressure of a deadline! We have many things to do; and many things on our minds. But nothing is there so constantly as the knowledge that we will preach on Sunday.

If not on the surface of our consciousness, it is always there in the background. Those who are wise decide early what to preach about and will have read the Scripture days ahead. Thus our conscious and unconscious minds are alerted to the subject, and can work on it intermittently. Some ministers work weeks ahead on sermons.

As we move through the week, we may be visiting homes, going to meetings, planning programs, catching up on correspondence, dealing with problems, going to school, or working as a tentmaking minister; but without fail a busy little signal in the back of our heads reminds us of that sermon.

It alerts us to an illustration we may read in the newspaper, or a need we discover in someone's life, or a problem we need to address, or an idea we can use; all of which adds to the sermon which is cooking.

Although we pastors have many important roles to fill, and preaching may be pushed from the top of the list occasionally, in actuality, the sermon seems to take precedence over all other concerns as a week rolls by. In a real sense, we live for Sunday and the eleven o'clock hour.

Perhaps the reason for this is because we are dealing with life and death matters, with the Word of Life, with death and resurrection; without which there is no salvation. Also, now and then, if not every week, something is stirring in us which wants to be preached, and cannot be denied.

We hope and silently pray that it will go well, for we learn early we can fail. We prepare with anticipation and trepidation knowing that if God does not preach in and through us, the joy of the gospel will turn to sorrow; and though the people may be kind, they will go away disappointed. So much rides on that Sunday sermon! It obsesses us throughout the week.

However, success or failure fades before the imperative to preach which burns in us, and the next week we go through the same throes and joys of sermonizing; and in spite of the demands, we love it. This is what God called us to do; this is what we like to do; and woe to us if we do not do it! Woe, not because we, like slaves, are driven to the task; but that God has elected us to proclaim the gospel, and we live with no purpose otherwise. This is our call and destiny, our reason for being; and nothing else is enough.

This brings us now to consider preaching as a major role of ministry.

> The church is apostolic because God calls her into being through the proclamation of the gospel first entrusted to the apostles. The church thus is built on the apostolic message which is faithfully proclaimed by messengers who follow in the footsteps of the apostles.[1]

THE PURPOSE OF THIS CHAPTER

This is not to be a chapter on *how* to preach. That can come later. Rather, it concerns itself with out attitudes toward and approach to preaching, and what preaching is and is not. It will deal with questions like—What is preaching? Why do we preach? How important is it? How do we approach it? What kind of sermons are we to preach?

WHAT PREACHING IS NOT

Because of many erroneous ideas about preaching, we will deal first with what preaching is not. This will be a word of caution to be taken seriously.

Preaching is not instruction in doctrine. We are not called to indoctrinate which means, telling people what and how to think and believe. Preaching is not brainwashing. It is not propagandizing. We are dealing with more than data and logic. To become too heavily rational in preaching is to rob the gospel of its power. There are other settings in which we can deal in an educational way with the doctrine and polity of our particular heritage.

Preaching is not instruction in morals. We are not called to moralize, which means, telling people dogmatically what they ought and ought not to do. Morals are deduced from the gospel. The gospel comes first. A wise old minister once said that he was not interested in telling people how to behave; he thought if they accepted the gospel that would be worked out later.

Moralizing on the part of many preachers has put preaching in a bad light. You have heard it said, "Don't preach at me!" as if preaching were distasteful. A certain kind of preaching is. We have not been called to sit in judgment on people's behavior; however, we *are* responsible for helping them interpret right and wrong in the light of the gospel. There is a difference. This is usually done through the teaching ministry of the church, but can be done in a sermon.

Preaching is not oratory—the use of flowery and scintillating words and phrases which often contain nothing but air. The gospel is better suited to simple everyday, working words of life than the airy and vacuous words of a charlatan; or the high-flown language of one who is trying to impress the congregation with one's vocabulary.

---

[1] *The Confession of Faith,* 5.05, Page 12

Preaching is not showmanship—entertaining people by dramatics, antics and a put-on voice and manner of speech. We are not called to entertain or to show off, but to let God speak the truth through a real person. A rather mild, but repugnant example of put-on is the holy tone some preachers use, as if they have to be one person in the pulpit and another outside.

Preaching is not lecturing. It is not providing information on a particular subject, even the Bible. A Bible lecture, or study, is not a sermon. Preaching surely will include information but it goes far beyond knowledge and facts.

Preaching is not a harangue. It is not scolding people for their failures, though at times we must confront ourselves and others concerning our wilful faults. Preaching is not taking our frustrations out on the people. The gospel is positive and full of hope.

Dr. H. H. Farmer says it very well in these words:

> A sermon is not *an essay* in which you give utterance to your views and impressions of life, though it could hardly fail to contain in some measure your views and impressions of life. It is not *a theological lecture*, though it will contain theology, and the sounder the theology the better. It is not *a discussion of political and social and international matters*, though that will surely not be absent. It is not *instruction in Christian morals*, though that will surely not be absent.[2] (Emphasis added)

WHAT PREACHING IS

We can simply say that preaching is the *proclamation of the gospel.*

> Whenever Christians worship, the gospel is to be proclaimed. The gospel means good news and is centered in what God has revealed to humankind throughout history, especially God's ultimate revelation in Jesus Christ. In worship Christians both announce and hear that good news of God's love, grace, judgment, reconciliation, forgiveness, mercy, and God's gracious call to service.[3]

> In the NT we find three words used: [concerning preaching] *euangelizesthai*, to preach good tidings, *katangellein*, to declare, announce, and *kerussein*, to proclaim as a herald. The fundamental idea of these words is the telling of news to people who had not heard it before—'evangelization.'... The apostolic church possessed a definite kerugma (lit. 'thing preached,' 'proclamation,' from *kerussein*). This kerugma underlies every book in the NT; it is the apostolic gospel. It is the Church's saving proclamation...This *kerugma* may be summed up in a word as the message of the cross and resurrection of Jesus Christ.[4,5]

---

[2] *The Servant of the Word,* H. H. Farmer, Scribners, 1942, page 16

[3] *The Confession of Faith,* page 83 (3)

[4] *A Theological Word Book of the Bible,* Alan Richardson, Macmillan, pp. 171, 172, under the topic, "Preach, Teach"

[5] Examples of apostolic preaching: Acts 2:14-39; 3:11-26; 7:2-53; 10:34-43; 13:16-41; 17:22-31; 22:1-21; 26:2-29

Further, in the New Testament *word* is almost always the translation of *logos* and *rhema*, Greek nouns, derived from verb roots meaning *to say*. The *Word* which we are to preach is what God has said to us in Jesus Christ. In a real sense, Jesus Christ *is the Word*. God speaks the *Word* through us. The Bible is the record of the Mighty Acts of God. It contains the *Word*. It is our basic resource.[6]

> Authentic preaching is a dynamic presentation of what God has done from the beginning, what he has done through the Man of Nazareth, our crucified and risen Lord, and what he is doing now...
> Authentic preaching is a celebration of God-given victory over the crises of life—be they crises of sin and separation or the crises of failure, suffering and loss...
> To preach is to become a part of a dynamic event wherein the living, redeeming God reproduces his act of redemption in a living encounter with persons through the preacher.[7]

Dr. James D. Smart reminds us that the ministry of Jesus Christ, into which we enter, is before all else the ministry of the word of God and as such a ministry of the spoken and written word. It is not the ministry of the preacher's word. He cautions us not to use the sermon as a means of our religious self-expression, asserting merely our own ideas and opinions. Although we preach out of our own experience of the gospel, and our knowledge of it, our primary task is to preach the Word God has spoken to us in Jesus Christ. Otherwise, we may be guilty of blasphemy by inserting our egotistical selves where only God and the Word should be.[8]

It should also be said here that we must be careful not to confuse the content of our own personal religious knowledge and experience with the whole gospel, and the Word of God. Although much, or even most or all, of this might be good and real to us, it is incomplete and limited. It is not *the* gospel or *the* Word. It is only what we have heard, learned, experienced and perceived; none of which is the whole truth. It has to be brought into the light of the gospel so we can see it for what it is.

> He does not preach himself, and he is not, therefore, at the mercy of his own moods, or even his experience. He is not compelled to preach only what he has made his own perfectly; he can turn the eyes of his people to Christ, whose riches are unsearchable. He is releasing a power of which he knows something, of which he nor any man can know all.[9]

Each congregation and community come to view religion in a certain way and it bears the stamp of human interpretation upon it. We must scrutinize it in the light of the truth that is in Jesus Christ. This is not to put down anyone's religious heritage; it is only to insist that it is not complete and whole. Many preachers succumb to the temptation to preach the content of their own particular religious

---

[6] *The Confession of Faith*, 1.04-1.07, pages 1, 2

[7] *Preaching and Pastoral Care*, Arthur L. Teikmanis, Fortress, 1964, pp. 17, 18

[8] *The Rebirth of Ministry*, James D. Smart, Westminster, 1978, pages 66 ff

[9] *Christian Worship*, E. Shillito, edited by N. Micklem, Oxford, Page 222

culture, thinking it is *the* Word. One excellent reason for continuous education is to help us come to know ourselves better and to have doors opened for growth and enlightenment.

Here is another interesting insight into the nature of preaching and worship as shared by Douglas Steere many years ago.

> Soren Kierkegaard in his penetrating devotional address, *Purity of Heart*, suggests that most Protestant church attenders act as if the church were a theater, where they are the critical audience and where the minister is the actor whose art they are expected to enjoy and to criticize. The situation in a church where the attenders have found their real relationship, Kierkegaard points out, is a very different one. The stage is there still, but now the attenders are upon it. They are the actors. The audience is there too—God is the audience. The preacher is there also, but he is inconspicuous in the scene. He is only the prompter. He is behind the wings whispering the text that they as the actors are speaking aloud before God. The responsibility has shifted here, and the relation between preacher and congregation has shifted too. They are collaborators now. He is their helper. He furnishes a text by which they may examine themselves before God. Here is a new attitude toward worship. It has become an occasion for coming more consciously into the presence of God and of reviewing our lives under His loving scrutiny.[10] (See pages 180, 187, *Purity of Heart*.)

Let us look again at some pertinent insights on preaching from Dr. H. H Farmer.

> Preaching is telling me something. But it is not merely *telling* me something. It is God actively probing me, challenging my will, calling on me for decision, offering me His succor, through the only medium which the nature of His purpose permits Him to use, the medium of a personal relationship. It is as though, to adopt the Apostle's words, 'God did beseech me by you'...
>
> Herein also appears the reason why preaching is sometimes called, in a broad sense, a *sacrament*. For while preaching is the preacher's activity, is the preacher saying something, yet it is only distinctively preaching in so far as it is uttered and listened to in the faith, however baffling the thought may be, that it is God's activity, that it is God encountering human souls in what may at any moment prove to be the supreme crisis of their life...[11]

Dr. Farmer goes on to say that though God uses the foolishness of preaching, we are responsible for seeing that it is not more foolish than it need be and that we are to bring our uttermost best to our preparation in order for it to be a redeeming means God can use.

From experience we can say without hesitation that a sermon which does not require time, energy, struggle, suffering, prayer, openness to God, and the needs of people on our hearts, is no sermon worthy of the name. Sermons come only out of the struggle of our souls to hear what God is trying to say through us to a particular group of people in a particular time and place. Sermon preparation calls for as much discipline as inspiration. God will not prepare our sermons for us. That

---

[10] *Prayer and Worship*, Douglas V. Steere, Association, 1938, Pages 46, 47
[11] *The Servant of the Word*, H. H. Farmer, Scribners, 1942, pp. 15, 16

is up to us. We do, however, claim the guidance of the Holy Spirit, for without this we cannot know the truth.

In sermonizing we look for resources everywhere, and borrow ideas from others; but God forbid that we substitute canned sermons, stolen or purchased outlines, for the discipline of hard work done in God's name and for the sake of the people.

Preaching is a fascinating, dynamic activity. If done well, it is a powerful means for change. When we preach we are interacting with the Word, ideas, the Holy Spirit, the people and ourselves. We have tried to listen as the Word has spoken to us and we are now relating that Word to the people in their condition and situation. We believe that the Holy Spirit is seeking to preach through us; our part is to be open.

We are using our voice not only to enable everyone to hear what is said, but also to express the message appropriately and effectively, letting it rise and fall, giving emphasis to certain words, lifting the voice when feeling moves us, and letting it drop into conversational tones as we try to relate intimately to the listeners. We should never speak in a monotone, for that connotes that what we are saying is dull and of the same value, and not very important.

We use our bodies when we get into the message, making gestures, using our hands to punch over some points, or to indicate the coming of God to our lives; or as a plea to hear. We move about some, for who can stand still when the good news is being proclaimed? The adrenalin is flowing and the heartbeat quickens. We look in people's eyes, letting our facial expressions say something to them, trying to make each one feel the sermon is for him or her.

We are involved and are involving the people so that they participate in the preaching. Our whole being is brought into preaching—intellect, emotion, will—as we appeal to the people in such a way as to cause them to think, feel and act.

Can we think of any other transaction which calls forth the whole person so much and involves so many as does the process of communicating the gospel through a sermon?

If we preach well, the people's interest is caught and held, and they listen as one. Some will listen better than others, though, because we are touching a nerve. We focus on those who are responding and look them in the eye. This adds to the dynamics of the interaction. It is part of the feedback essential to intercommunication.

We do not want to leave the impression that we have to use oratory and soar in voice and feeling in order to preach. It can be done conversationally. In fact, the most effective preaching today seems to be conversational, for it is a means by which we can communicate personally to people. But even in a conversation, all those things mentioned in preaching can be brought into use. Good conversations are never dull and can involve a lot of thinking and feeling; and sometimes a lot of gesturing and eyeballing.

How do the concepts of preaching presented in this section strike you? Can you identify with some of the ideas?

WHY PREACH?

Just as we need to understand what preaching is, so do we need to know why we do it. The *why* is just as important as the *what*.

What is our *motivation* for preaching?

We preach because the church has been commissioned by God through Jesus Christ to preach the gospel, and has put preaching first.

> Go into all the world and preach the gospel to the whole creation.[12]

> Repentance and forgiveness of sin should be preached in his name to all nations, beginning from Jerusalem.[13]

We preach because we as individuals have been called to preach. God has put the urge and the imperative in us to do so.

We preach because we believe the gospel is the true source of salvation and wholeness for humankind. We believe that although God has spoken to people in and through other religions, God has spoken the redeeming word to us uniquely in Jesus Christ.

> In many and various ways God spoke of old to our fathers by the prophets; but in these last days he has spoken to us by a Son, whom he appointed the heir of all things, through whom also he created the world.[14]

> For "every one who calls upon the name of the Lord will be saved." But how are they to call on one in whom they have not believed? And how are they to believe in one of whom they have never heard? And how are they to hear without someone to proclaim him? And how are they to proclaim him unless they are sent? As it is written "How beautiful are the feet of those who bring good news."[15]

We preach because God's approach to men and women is usually through other persons. God uses us to move into the lives of others. The sermon is a specific way in a certain time and place to do it. One basic assumption we have as Christians is that God is always seeking us out and will use many ways to find us. The sermon is one way. Because of this, the sermon is of decisive importance and requires our very best.

What is the *purpose* of our preaching? In a nutshell, we preach to inform, interpret, challenge, stir, move, convict, convert, change, save, reconcile and encourage.

> In worship Christians both announce and hear that good news of God's love, grace, judgment, reconciliation, forgiveness, mercy, and God's gracious call to service.[16]

We preach to help people grow, to guide them in their living. "To set forth a road map for life." (J. Keith Cook)

---

[12] Mark 16:15 RSV

[13] Luke 24:47 RSV

[14] Hebrews 1:1, 2 RSV

[15] Romans 10:13-15 NRSV

[16] *Confession of Faith*, page 83 (3), last sentence

> To equip the saints for the work of ministry, for building up the body of Christ, until we all attain to the unity of the faith and of the knowledge of the Son of God, to maturity, to the measure of the stature of the fullness of Christ.[17]

We preach to create faith in the future, and hope, for those who hear and for the world.

> For whatever was written in former days was written for our instruction, that by steadfastness and by the encouragement of the scriptures we might have hope.[18]

> Thy kingdom come, Thy will be done, On earth as it is in heaven.[19]

We also preach to develop a Christian conscience. We may not be able to change all the ills of the world; but we can appeal to an unconsenting conscience and help people think and feel as Jesus did about human beings and their need for justice, love, and reconciliation, and invite them to action.

> How much more will the blood of Christ, who offered himself, blameless as he was, to God through the eternal Spirit, purify our conscience from dead actions so that we can worship [serve] the living God.[20]

In our preaching, we seek the active participation of the listeners. We are not merely trying to inform or to entertain; we preach for action and decision. The sermon is to point to some goal or challenge which calls for the people to respond in action.

> So then, my brothers and sisters, because of God's great mercy to us I appeal to you: Offer yourselves as a living sacrifice to God, dedicated to his service and pleasing to him.[21]

Although most ministers like to hear the people say at the door, "I enjoyed your sermon," this is not the purpose for preaching. It may need to be the opposite. For we preach also to disturb, to arouse, to waken and to point to matters which need to be righted.

> "These men who have turned the world upside down have come here also..."
> And the people and the city authorities were disturbed when they heard this."[22]

---

[17] Ephesians 4:12, 13 RSV

[18] Romans 15:4

[19] Matthew 6:10 RSV

[20] Hebrews 9:14 Jerusalem Bible

[21] Romans 12:1 TEV

[22] Acts 17:6c, 8

WILL WE BE PROPHETIC, PASTORAL, OR PRIESTLY PREACHERS?

It is suggested by one author that ministers need to consider whether they will be prophetic, pastoral or priestly preachers.[23] He suggests that we will be all three some of the time, but that for the most part we will choose one and stay with it.

We will review now the meaning of these terms—prophet, pastor, priest— in order to help us decide the kind of preacher we want to be. *The prophet* is to proclaim the Word of God as it applies to the *total* life of the people. That includes all areas of our society, nation and world. He speaks for God and declares God's will and way, dealing with the current issues of the day.

The Old Testament prophets are examples. They often got themselves stoned because those being addressed thought the prophets were meddling in something which was none of their business. The attitude still holds today, to a large extent. We are divided on whether the gospel concerns itself only with personal salvation and Christian growth; or whether it is a gospel of social responsibility and witness in a sinful world; and whether we ought to preach on social, economic and environmental matters. It needs to be said clearly that prophetic preaching should be done in a pastoral context, and not dogmatically. It should insist that the church address itself in Christ's name to anything which affects people's lives, and that to do so demands prayer, thought, study and research.

The *pastor* cares for the needs of the people, meeting them where they are and not where "they should be." They relate personally to the people, caring, guiding and counseling. (See Chapter 4 of this book.)

The *priest* is the representative of the people before God, the mediator between the two. The priest takes care of the rituals of the church, acting also as the caretaker of the institution, preserving its traditions and heritage.

Priestly preachers may assure the people and lead them to God, stressing God's Providence, and continuing love. They may interpret the gospel in the light of traditions.

We will probably be prophetic, pastoral or priestly according to our own inclinations, and the needs which we see. However, there is an interrelatedness in all three, and each informs and complements the other. It is probable that we will switch from one to another as we proceed in our ministry. The matter of choosing between the three is left to the individual minister. Each is authentic and legitimate and has its place.[24]

As has already been said, this chapter is not offering instruction on how to preach. That belongs to another stage in our education. However, there are some things we need to know regarding our approach to preaching. The attitude with which we regard and practice preaching is highly important and will, to a great degree, determine the outcome of our efforts. The following pages will deal with these matters.

---

[23] *The First Parish*, J. Keith Cook, Westminster, 1983, Pages 76 ff.

[24] For a brief but helpful treatment of the three kinds of preaching, see *The First Parish*, Cook, Pages 76-79.

SOME GENERAL GUIDELINES ON PREACHING

Preach in the context of worship. Public worship is not just a preaching service, though the sermon is a large part of it. Many people think of going to preaching, instead of going to worship. The sermon is important to them. It is the one time in the week when they hear God's Word, and they hunger for it.

A regular churchgoer, complaining of all the responses and other parts of ritual through which they went in her church, said, "They nearly wear us out before they get to the sermon." There is no doubt about what she thought was important. We affirm with her that the sermon *is* significant.

The sermon, however, must not be separate from other parts of the service. Preaching is an integral element of worship. Although the earlier movements in the service may help prepare us for the sermon, they are not just preliminary to it. They have meaning within themselves. The entire liturgy should blend into a whole. Worship and preaching must be unified. The hymns, prayers and responses are essential, but we want a sermon also. On the other hand, while we enjoy and need a good sermon, it would not mean so much without the liturgy. How could we preach and hear without having our hearts warmed and prepared beforehand?

Preach with urgency. True preaching *will* be done imperatively. If the gospel is true, we ought to be excited about it. If it is good news to those who need it, we should be telling it with great enthusiasm. How can we be cool and indifferent in the presence of troubled lives, if we have at hand what can bring deliverance? We who preach need to pray that God will help us internalize the crises before us. Do we really believe people have no hope without Christ? Are we aware that for some who hear the time is now for decision and response? A comprehension of this fact will add power to our preaching.

Preach to give hope and encouragement. The Word is always full of hope. Sermons ought to resolve conflict and guilt, not cause them. The gospel always says, "You can do better with Christ's help." The message should enable people to find ways out of their moral, spiritual and social dilemmas.

In spite of this, there are still those among us who feel they have not been helped unless the preacher *hits* them, whatever that means. On the positive side, it may mean that the homily applied to some problem or need. It found its mark. On the negative side, it may mean that they want to be scolded because they deserve it, and it relieves them to be whipped. Or, it may mean they don't feel we have preached unless we censure them. In some cases, this kind of preaching seems to become entertainment and some are happy when we are pouring it on them. There is probably some psychology at work here, which we do not understand.

Nevertheless, Christian preachers are not called to manhandle the congregation, but to point to salvation.

Preach within the pastoral relationship. This enables us to preach with understanding and helpfulness. If we relate pastorally to the people, living in their lives and hearing their stories, we will better communicate the Word to their lives. Otherwise, we will be dealing largely with ideas unrelated to their situation; or will be hard or indifferent toward their problems. True pastors preach in a caring way. The people come to feel we understand them, and that they really matter. The longer we are in the pastorate the more we will come to see the importance of pastoral preaching. Kind and acceptive clergy preach by their presence even more than they do by their sermons. The message of love is embodied.

Preach to the needs of the people. There are basic needs which we all have: love, acceptance, assurance, security, strength, encouragement, forgiveness, forgivingness, hope, peace, and a sense of God in our lives.

There are situational needs also. They arise out of our relationships and circumstances. They include such things as being Christian at work, handling sorrow, dealing with doubt, living under stress, overcoming addictions, loneliness, failure, anger, and many more.

> All preaching is preaching to personal needs, if it is really preaching and not the delivery of an essay or a general address to nobody in particular or mere vocal muscle flexing.[25]

> A questionnaire, seeking answers at this level, queried the person in the pew. The purpose was to find out what people want from their pastors through their sermons. About half of the 4,000 queried indicated a concern about intensely personal matters, such as the futility of life, insecurity in personal relations, a haunting sense of loneliness, problems that involve marriage and the proper control of sex drives, the effect of alcohol, false ideas of religion and morals, a feeling if inferiority, the problem of suffering as well as the problem of illness, and the feeling of guilt and frustration. Another fourth of those who responded were concerned about family problems...[26]

> I ask the congregation to list the two or three sermons they remember most. Inevitably they remember the sermons that deal with prayer, suffering, marriage, the Commandments, death, worry, forgiveness—the things of which every day life is made.[27]

Preach prophetically. This is said in spite of what is written above. It is impossible to escape preaching to all of life if we are concerned for the welfare of persons. Anything which affects the life of human beings is our concern. The kind of society which we have created produces countless problems for us. Think of the misery and confusion of many whom we know, who have been influenced by the kind of world we live in, especially the young who are growing up in it! How can we keep silent about it?

How can we not speak in Christ's name about war and peace, racial discrimination, justice, poverty, drugs, economics, AIDS, sex and the breakdown of sexual standards, liberation of men and women, education, abortion, marriage and divorce, politics and politicians, government, creation and environment and health care in the light of human tragedies all about us? Can we ignore the world? Has Christ no word at all to speak to it? Has he no compassion for those who suffer?

If we believe the Bible, God not only called the prophets, but spoke through them to the sinful conditions of the era. Social, economic, and religious problems were, and are, God's concern. If God called us, God called us to be priests, pastors,

---

[25] *Dynamic Preaching*, James W. Clarke, Revell, 1960, page 65
[26] *A Psychology for Preaching*, Edgar N. Jackson, Channel, 1961, Page 75
[27] *The First Parish*, J. Keith Cook, Westminster, 1983, Page 79

and prophets. Then, will we not, like Jeremiah, cry to God, "there is in my heart as it were a burning fire shut up in my bones, and I am weary with holding it in, and I cannot"?[28]

"And yet, and yet," we ask, "What can we say? Who will hear? Where can we take hold of this monolith of concerns? It is so complex so complicated, so big—where can we begin? Anyway, can we hope to change things?"

No one is quite capable of counseling us on prophetic preaching. *Each* of us will have to work this out for *ourselves.* It should be done with fear and trembling. Great values, and our own integrity, are at stake.

Some things should be kept in mind as we decide.

First, whatever prophetic preaching we do should be done in a pastoral context, that is, out of a heart that cares. It must be done out of sincere interest in people and their welfare.

Second, it must be done out of knowledge and understanding of the issues. This comes out of observance, study, research, and discussion. We had better know what we are talking about for we will be harshly questioned.

Third, our sermons should not be proposals of solutions. Who has the answers? Let them be an appeal to address the situation and seek to hear what God has to say about it.

Fourth, let us remember that there are scriptural resources to guide us. Read the prophets. Remember also that Jesus himself was unafraid to tackle the entrenched power in the temple and drive the moneychangers out of it. He also preached scathing sermons to those who were a part of the evil.[29] He was crucified by Rome, as a troublemaker, having disturbed the Empire. And did not the apostles bring fury down upon their heads by upsetting the status quo?

Some ministers and congregations provide opportunities for the study and discussion of current issues. Evidently only a small minority of church members show an interest.

In a very real sense, being prophetic is not a matter of choice, though it is a dilemma for many. We need to be thoughtful and prayerful about it.

However, the fact is that the gospel is never the gospel in isolation, but always in relation to persons and "all creation."[30]

It is good news and needs to be told to all the world. The good news is that we are all equal in God's sight, that God wills peace, that we are called to love one another, that justice must roll down like waters, that everyone deserves the basic needs of life, that sin will be punished but can be forgiven, that the way of Jesus is the true way, that male and female are made for each other, that the truth will set us free, that life is sacred, that marriage is holy, that the strong ought to help the weak, that we are our brothers' and sisters' keepers, and that in Christ the whole world can be saved, for "God so loved the world that he sent his son..."

Preach humbly. Is the preacher an authority, or a resource? Do we think people ought to listen to us and believe every word? Do we think we are preaching the true and complete Word when we speak? Or do we think that the Holy Spirit speaks to and through others also?

---

[28] Jeremiah 20:9

[29] See Matthew 23

[30] Mark 16:15; Matthew 28:19

The Holy Spirit can and does work in the people in the pew as well as in the person in the pulpit. Sermons are resources for the people to use in their journey of faith. They may use some of the sermon, but seldom all of it. They do not have to agree with us for the sermon to help them. If it stimulates them to thought and action it has been successful.

It may help us to remember that we not only preach *to* the people; we preach *for* them. We are their representatives as well as God's. They have called us to preach the gospel in their congregation. It is a partnership. They need us and we need them.

Preach in the vernacular (The language of the people). We ministers tend to want to be unique. We would like to feel we are the answer to the need for brilliant and clever sermons. In spite of the seriousness of our calling, there is a little bit of *ham* in all of us. We would like to think we are much better preachers than we really are. The word *ham* is slang for "a poor actor or performer who plays in an effected or exaggerated fashion," trying to convince others that she or he is a star. We would like each sermon to be a masterpiece, and the subject matter something no one ever preached, or preached so well, and in such exquisite vocabulary!

Dr. John Killinger, in an article in *The Presbyterian Outlook*, picked up on a phrase from a drama and related it to preaching. The phrase is "The public is convervative." This is what he had to say.

> The sermons that touch people most profoundly are not the cleverest, most original ones—the ones that would have gladdened the heart of a seminary homiletics professor—but the ones that say essentially what people expect to hear, that take the old, familiar themes and present them with just a soupcon [a slight amount] of freshness and rearrangement. Congregations don't give a lot of points for inventiveness...
>
> I began to concentrate on hitting the great diapason notes people have heard before and have come to expect as part of the full instrumentation of their faith.[31]

Preach in Correct English. Preaching is communication. It is the communication of the greatest truth known to us. It should be done in the most correct and proper language. Incorrect usage of language detracts from the sermon. Even the children notice it.

Unfortunately some of us were reared in homes in which incorrect English was spoken. We picked up on it. Others of us did not do well in English and grammar, and we never learned how to speak accurately. Hence, when we preach we make grammatical errors.

All of us can learn to speak good English, if we set our minds to it, and think it is important. It is a matter of taking time and getting someone to teach us. This is essential to effective preaching. *How* we say something is almost as important as *what* we say. They go together.

Most of us grow careless in speech. We need a coach to keep us on track. Spouses can fill this role. Or, if not, ministers can select someone quietly from the congregation to work with them in this task.

---

[31] *The Presbyterian Outlook,* Issue of April 29, 1985, page 10. "St. Agatha and the Preacher," John Killinger.

Preach with empathy. Feel *with*, not merely *for* others. Identify with them. Include ourselves with the congregation. Use *we*, not *you*. We are one with each other. We are all sinners, or sinners saved grace. We stand on level ground before the cross. We preachers are not holier people who can preach high above the people. We are a part of them.

Father Damien, who went to Molokai to preach to the lepers there, became effective when he discovered he had contracted the dreadful disease. He began his next sermon with, "We lepers."

Preach with freedom. The freedom of the pulpit is as essential as our other freedoms; otherwise, we will be kept persons, like prostitutes, employed to satisfy the whims and sanctify the prejudices of the people.

In spite of what has been said here about preaching to the needs of the congregation and sharing the responsibility of preaching with the people, and whether we are authorities or not, let us affirm our right to preach our honest convictions (not just our opinions) which have grown out of commitment, observation, study, living, prayer, and mature thinking.

One of the first things which should be agreed upon, or understood, in forming a pastoral relation is whether or not the pulpit is free. Maybe we can assume that it is. In spite of our need to use good judgment, and to consider the feelings of others and not go overboard or to extremes; and in spite of the fact that the people are to be given the right to think for themselves, we must accept the responsibility of speaking for God and claim our right as a called person to preach the Word in its fullest meaning. We have been commissioned.

Why else were we called? Why else were we called to a particular congregation? Were we called to leave the people where they are, or to lead them toward a fuller obedience to God's will?

But while we are saying this, let us add that if we claim the freedom of the pulpit, we had better be sure of our credentials. Are we willing to discipline ourselves to prayer and study so that we can command (or earn) authority by our integrity and thoroughness, and not go off half-cocked on every issue?

Still further, here is a word to the young, immature or beginning minister, who may still be in school, or who has started preaching before ordination, as well as to the rest of us. If we are young and inexperienced, or somewhat uninformed about the world and the issues we face, and the comprehensive meanings of our faith, we had better use our freedom carefully. To speak for God is to do our best to find what God wants us to say. God probably has much more for us to say than we have yet discovered, or that God has given us.

> I have yet many things to say to you, but you cannot bear them now.[32]

And, in spite of our call and response, where did we get the audacity to think we know how to speak for God? This big job of ours calls always for humility and self-examination to prevent our talking nonsense, jumping to conclusions, echoing what we have heard someone else say, or spouting preconceived notions.

Now if a little ego voice pipes up and says, "But I'm preaching the Bible," the answer is for all of us: Because we are limited and human, we are preaching *our*

---

[32] John 16:12

interpretation of the Bible; and it is never the full truth. (O God, even at our best we are humble and limited servants of yours!)

Now someone may protest: "Then, who on earth can preach or have the nerve to try?" Well, God called us. God must think we can learn. The Holy Spirit is with us. We must rely on God to lead us with cords of love and patience.

> We have this treasure in earthen vessels, to show the transcendant power belongs to God and not to us.[33]

Preach from the Lectionary. (A sequence or list of Scriptures to be read and preached in church services during the year.)[34] Each lesson in the Lectionary is assigned to be helpful on a particular Lord's Day within the Christian year.

> A lectionary not only aids worshipers in the remembering of the events of God but also assures the reading and the hearing of the Old Testament and the New Testament in their fullness... This lectionary provides readings for a cycle of three years.[35]

> Sermons are based upon scripture and shaped by scripture. In preparing sermons it is necessary to be guided by *all* of scripture in order that *all* aspects of the gospel will be proclaimed. Orderly selection of scripture passages upon which those preaching base their sermons, such as some form of lectionary, is encouraged.[36] (emphasis added)

The lectionary provides a balanced list of scriptures and over a period of years we will have covered a variety of passages and not merely preached our favorites. In preaching from these scriptures we find that they address themselves to a wide diversity of needs and situations and we will have covered many important themes.

If we resist with the insistence that we are going to let the Holy Spirit lead us to themes and scriptures, we may consider the possibility that the

---

FOR FURTHER CONSIDERATION

- Can you think of some problems related to your approach to preaching which this chapter has not considered?

- Evaluate your preaching in the light of some guidelines given here. How would you rate yourself?

- Think about the meaning of prophetic, pastoral and priestly preaching. Which kind do you do? Why?

- Read the examples of apostolic preaching given in the footnote on page 77.

- Write down the major points. What do you see as being the major content of these sermons?

- Think of three sermons you choose at random which you have preached in the past year. Measure them by the definition of what preaching is in this chapter.

- To what extend are you preaching the Word?

---

[33] II Corinthians 4:7

[34] See *The Book of Common Worship*, 1946, pp. 376-388, Westminster and *The Worshipbook*, 1970, pp. 166-175, Westminster.

[35] *The Worshipbook*, 1970, page 166, Westminster

[36] *The Confession of Faith*, Directory for Worship, Frontier, Page 86 (5)

Holy Spirit led in the selection of those in the Lectionary.

The Lectionary is a good discipline in keeping our preaching Bible centered, and in confronting us with the need to study passages which we might otherwise pass over, but which offer us an opportunity to preach the gospel in its fullness. If, on some weeks, we find the passages difficult and seemingly irrelevant or hard to interpret, we may look at this as a challenge to deeper Bible research and study.

To recommend the Lectionary for use is not to say we cannot depart from it on occasions when the need and opportunity appear. There are events current in the world which demand attention which the Lectionary may not give. Dire needs may become very evident in the life of the people calling for other scripture than that provided in the reading for the day. We must keep ourselves free to turn elsewhere for a biblical resource. However, we are suggesting that the Lectionary may be used over a period of time in an effort to see how it serves us in preaching during the Christian year. It will save us from many pitfalls and will relieve us of the task of finding appropriate themes week after week.

CHAPTER 7
The Pastor as Teacher and Educator

WE ARE TEACHERS

The gifts he gave were that some would be...pastors and teachers, to equip the saints for the work of ministry, for building up the body of Christ.[1]

Many who are called into the ministry regard preaching as their only task and forget other roles such as teaching. When we respond to God's call, we enter into the ministry of Jesus Christ. We take our cue from him, and we continue the ministry he began on earth. Among other things he was known as "a teacher come from God."[2] We also trace the ministry through the Old and New Testament and see that teaching was one of the major roles.

WHAT THE BIBLE SAYS

There is much biblical evidence that teaching was an important work in Old Testament times. Dueteronomy 6 is a good example, and still is a guide for us. Proverbs is full of instruction, and indicates the importance of the teaching function of the home. The prophets were both preachers and teachers. Many of them gathered groups of learners to be trained in the faith and to be sent out to preach and teach.[3] Following the Exile, scribes became teachers. Ezra is a good example.

The role of teaching continued in the New Testament Church. As we know, Jesus was called teacher. Mark describes him as one who was constantly teaching. The letters of Paul to Timothy stress the importance of teaching. Paul lists teachers among those who are of most importance in ministry. From the very beginning of

---

[1] Ephesians 4:11c, 12 NRSV

[2] John 3:2 RSV

[3] Nehemiah 8:1-8

the church in Jerusalem the apostles taught those who were being brought into the faith.

WHAT OUR CONFESSIONS SAY

The Cumberland Presbyterian Church has served under the guidance of three *Confessions of Faith*— those of 1814, 1883 and 1984. All three have stressed the importance of educational ministry of the church and the responsibilities of the pastor and session in administering it. We will quote from the most recent.

> Responsibility for the government of a particular church belongs to the session...The session thus constituted is responsible to lead the members in all those ministries which belong to the church...[which include]:
> Christian education, including study of the scriptures for Christian growth...[4]
>
> The person who fills the office of the ministry has in the scriptures, different titles, expressive of various duties: [included is]
> Teacher—who explains the scriptures emphasizing the lessons essential to Christian growth.[5]
>
> The session is charged with pastoral oversight of the particular church and has the responsibility to: [included is]
> Establish and give oversight to church schools, Bible classes, fellowship and other organizations within the church, with special attention being given to nurture of children...[6]
>
> Prior to ordination the licentiate shall sustain a careful and satisfactory examination by the committee on the ministry and presbytery as a whole upon the following... [included is]
> ...the educational task of the church...[7]

DO WE HAVE AN APTNESS TO TEACH?

Perhaps a word about the difference between preaching and teaching will be of help. Preaching is proclamation of the gospel. Teaching addresses itself to the task of helping people understand the faith and to respond to it, and guiding them in their Christian growth afterward. Continuous teaching is essential as persons grow from stage to stage in a world that changes constantly, in which standards and values are always in a state of flux.

In Paul's first letter to Timothy he names some qualifications of the bishop (overseer, shepherd), among which is an aptness to teach.[8] We vary in our strengths and talents. We are stronger in some roles than in others. We need to ask

---

[4] *Confession of Faith*, 1984, Constitution, Section 2.51, Page 28

[5] Ibid., Constitution, Section 2.62, Page 30

[6] Ibid., Constitution, Section 4.5, Page 40

[7] Ibid., Constitution, Section 6.32, Page 49

[8] I Timothy 3:2 NRSV

ourselves if we have an aptness to teach, or if we can learn to be a teacher.

Teachers instruct and inform, elicit (bring forth), stimulate, correct, guide, interpret and model what they teach. Pastor-teachers do so to lead unbelievers to Christ; to enable believers to fulfil their discipleship; and to develop Christians for the work of ministry. Like Paul, they agonize over the process of molding the learners into the shape of Christ's spirit, attitude, thought and way of life.

> For my children you are, and I am in travail with you over again until you take the shape of Christ.[9]

WHEN AND WHERE WE TEACH

A list of teaching opportunities, as given below, will enable us to see our teaching role more specifically. We can teach in the following ways:

A Sunday school class, if requested
Bible Study in small groups
In fellowship groups such as children, youth and adults
Special courses, like training Sunday school workers
Preaching
Counseling: dealing with problems, pre-marital and marital counseling, career counseling, etc.
Communicants' Classes (using resources like *Journey of Faith*, Frontier Press)
When doing pastoral work in relation to families and individuals
When people, anywhere and anytime, ask questions and seek information
In session meetings, and in classes and retreats with elders
In deacons' meetings, and discussion groups with deacons
Dialoging with CPW and Circles in learning and teaching situations

TEACHERS MUST BE LEARNERS

As teachers, we must be persistent and constant learners. The work of ministry demands that we be students: reading books and periodicals, attending conferences and seminars, learning from other ministers, listening to lay persons and gathering information and insights from many sources. We need to read the Bible daily. This is our main resource. The need to keep abreast of new developments calls us to read in the fields of history, literature, psychology, sociology, theology, education, communication, biography, and current fiction, which reflects the life of our world. There is no end to this demand and opportunity. It calls for discipline and the setting of schedules for this purpose.

Learning also means more than acquiring knowledge. It means change and growth. We cannot ever assume we have come to know enough about anything, or have arrived at maturity.

> Yet, my brothers, I do not consider myself to have "arrived," spiritually, nor do I consider myself already perfect. But I keep going on, grasping ever more firmly that purpose for which Christ grasped me. My brothers, I do not consider myself to have fully grasped it even now. But I do concentrate on this:

---

[9] Galatians 4:19 NEB

> I leave the past behind and with hands outstretched to whatever lies ahead
> I go straight for the goal—my reward the honour of being called by God in
> Christ.[10]

BUT MORE—WE ARE EDUCATORS

In addition to an already overwhelming set of roles, we ministers are also educators, or will need to learn to be. We, along with the other members of the session, are responsible for the Christian education programs of our congregation. This has already been established by the quotations from our *Confession of Faith* above. This fact impresses us with the need for much learning in order to succeed. The learning will be, in part, an orientation to this role. Perhaps we had not thought of ourselves as educators; persons in charge of an educational program for a church. Many pastors reject this work and turn it over to another professional, if the congregation can afford it, or to a layperson in the parish. Although ministers need much help in this area, and should share much of it with others, they should never relinquish the reins of the role to others. The pastor and elders, according to our *Confession of Faith*, are the ones upon whose shoulders this trust falls.

In order for us to see more fully what this means, we will discuss the nature of Christian education, its place in the church, and how the responsibility for it is to be carried out.

THE NATURE OF CHRISTIAN EDUCATION

Christian education has to do with spiritual growth toward maturity.

> Until all of us come to the unity of the faith and of the knowledge of the Son
> of God, to maturity, to the measure of the full stature of Christ.[11]

Spiritual growth is a complex process not yet fully understood by any of us. It is a part of the mystery of the gospel. It is initiated and sustained by the Holy Spirit and is to be nurtured by the church through Christian education. Christian education—as a plan for study, Christian nurture, and action in the church—is also *complicated*. It can never be simplified to the degree that many would like for it to be. It demands a lot of effort including study, reflection, and prayer. This is true whether we are planning, administering or teaching. It also requires a great deal of attention to detail. We either give this attention or we fail. It is at this point many leaders fall short. They have the vision and make plans but tend to leave the details of following through to others or to luck.

Christian education is of the essence of the church. It is not a mere addition or an option. It is central to the work and mission of Christianity. It is as essential as worship, preaching, the sacraments, pastoral care, outreach and administration. It is integrally related to all these.

---

[10] Philippians 3:12-14, Phillips

[11] Ephesians 4:13 NRSV

> The existence of Christian education as a distinct area of study and action in the church rests upon the assumption that the Church of Jesus Christ has, of necessity, a teaching function. The church must teach, just as it must preach, or it will not be the church...Teaching belongs to the essence of the church and the church that neglects this function of teaching has lost something that is indispensable to its nature as a church.[12]

Other writers and professionals in this field affirm this same belief.

A statement on the objective of Christian education, approved by the General Assembly of the Cumberland Presbyterian Church, helps us better understand its nature. It combines the best elements of evangelism, education and theology. It reflects the many dimensions of Christian education:

> The objective of Christian education is
> > to help persons
> > > to be aware of God's self-disclosure and seeking love in Jesus Christ, and
> >
> > to respond in faith and love
> > to the end that they may
> > > know who they are and what their human situation means,
> > > grow as children of God rooted in the Christian community,
> > > live in the Spirit of God in every relationship,
> > > fulfill their common discipleship in the world, and
> > > abide in the Christian hope.

This objective is a means of grace, for salvation and growth, mission and service. To think of it as a means of grace gives it a new aura.

> God has established a function of teaching in his church as well as a function of preaching, that his work of grace may take place, not just at one decisive moment in a [person's] life, but throughout the whole of it...[13]

> Teachers are "mediators of the grace and truth of God's ever creative and redemptive Word."[14]

The objective is a guide for all teaching. It helps us to see a broad scope of Christian education and to recognize that the church teaches formally and informally; in word and deed; and through relationships. The whole church teaches by its spirit and attitude, its atmosphere (physically and spiritually), what it does and does not do, how and why it does what it does, what it says intentionally, and what people (especially children) overhear it saying. It teaches through planned structures and settings such as Sunday school, organized classes, fellowship groups, the home and family and other such designs and systems.

---

[12] *The Teaching Ministry of the Church,* James D. Smart, Westminster, 1954, Page 11

[13] Ibid., Page 20

[14] *Teaching in the Community of Faith,* Charles R. Foster, Abingdon, 1982, Page 9

PRIMARY RESPONSIBILITY IN THE CONGREGATION

The session is primarily responsible for Christian education in the congregation. This includes the pastor, who is expected to take the lead. This charge entails initiating, planning, guiding and making Christian education effective. It may be delegated to a Board (or Committee) of Christian Education, a Task Force, or designated person or persons, selected by the Session, who are answerable to the session.[15] Whatever is done must be adjusted to the size and nature of the congregation.

SOME ROLE TASKS OF THE SESSION AND PASTOR

These tasks pertain to Christian education. There are others which concern the whole work of the church. These which are given may appear to be new and different by some sessions, and more inclusive of duties which have not heretofore been carried out. They are proposed on the assumption that sessions work, not just meet to exercise authority and power. If the session delegates this work of Christian education to some other group or persons like a board or committee, they will share these role tasks along with the session.

The pastor and elders are bridgebuilders. Generally, local congregations are a mixture of conservative and liberal views, of evangelical and educational approaches, of traditional and innovative attitudes, and probably more. The session cannot always stand pat on its own views and concepts. Adaptation may be necessary. It is faced with the job of bringing together the diverse elements into a working instrument. The pastor and elders are bridgebuilders.

They are also to build bridges between the congregation and the presbytery, the synod, and the General Assembly Boards of Christian Education, and other boards and agencies. These judicatory agencies are resources designed to help the congregation do its mission.

The pastor and elders are to be inquirers, learners and educators. In a real sense they are to serve as models of growth. They lead by what they are becoming as well as by what they say. They have to keep on learning if they are to make informed decisions. They cannot assume they already have the answers and that all they have to do is to apply them. Life changes, and they must keep abreast of the times and up with the trends. Churches cannot move toward maturity if leaders do not grow.

Christian education is done in a variable world. We serve in times of exodus and exile. Nothing ever remains the same. We cannot run in place and keep up. We all need to read books on Christian education, go to conferences, discuss what is going on with other pastors and elders. It is important to listen to lay people and try to understand what is going on with families, with children and youth, and with older people. It is imperative that we continue to learn all kinds of things if we are to be educators in this kind of world.

Sessions must learn to think as educators. This involves the consideration of the Bible, our theology, various age groups, objectives, goals, programs and curriculum materials, buildings and space, personnel and any other factor which

---

[15] For details on planning Christian education see *Christian Education Plan Book*, produced by the Federated Board of Christian Education. Order free from 1978 Union, Memphis, TN 38104.

influences the learning process in the church. We are in charge of an educational program.

Pastors and elders are to be innovators as well as conservers. It is assumed that the church is a conservative institution, maintaining and conserving Christian traditions in a changing world. Institutions tend to become conservative for their purpose is to maintain and promote certain values and concepts. In this sense sessions are to play the role of conservers.

But to be a conserver is not always what some think it to be. There are those who feel that to be conservative is to be against anything new; in spite of the fact that new plans and movements often create good values and preserve old and permanent ones.

To be an innovator is to propose and introduce new ideas and actions to meet the needs which arise out of the changes that are evolving in the world. It does not mean going out and doing or proposing radical and shocking things to attract attention or for novelty. In every congregation there is a need for something new and more effective. We all fall into the proverbial rut and follow the line of least resistance. Consequently, people lose interest and enthusiasm dies. We need to remember that the church is not only an institution. It was in the beginning a dynamic movement. In truth, it still is, or can be. It can be thought of as the Community of the Holy Spirit. The Holy Spirit brings fire upon the earth and will use any church that is open to the Power. If, in deed and in truth, we believe in the Holy Spirit and are willing to be obedient, there are many new directions we can take in the church which will be accepted and supported by the people if initiated properly by the leaders, and if it is perceived that the Holy Spirit is leading. Just as the Holy Spirit moved the early Christians out into the world with the good news, it is plausible to think that the Holy Spirit is trying to move us out into new fields of witness and work today.

New things for one church may not be new for others; and yet, may fill a need that has been existing, or is emerging, in the situation. We will propose some new departures that may be possible in many of our churches, and which could be in response to needs and the leadings of the Holy Spirit. They will be made in the form of questions, thus issuing a challenge.

>Why not organize a library or media center?
>Why not experiment with an intergenerational Sunday school class?
>Why not organize a class for singles?
>Why not hold a family retreat, or do some other program to aid families with their problems?
>Why not set up a schedule for leadership training?
>Why not appoint a Christian Education Committee, or provide some equivalent means for a new surge in Christian nurture?
>Why not evaluate the Sunday school literature the church is using? Is it the best for the congregation?[16]
>Is the church making adequate provisions for the nurture of its children?
>Why not organize the Third Agers in the congregation?[17]

---

[16] Order *curriculum guides* from Board of Christian Education to help you select the best literature for your Sunday school.

[17] See *Third Age Ministry in the Congregation,* 1990, Federated Board of Christian Education, Order from 1978 Union, Memphis, TN 38104, Free.

Why not lead the church in a self-study?[18]

Or why not set up a schedule of special classes for members of the congregation in such areas as follows, to be taught by the pastor (a teaching elder and the resident theologian), or by competent lay persons? Examples:

How the Bible Came to Be
The Mighty Acts of God (by Arnold Rhodes, an overview of the entire Bible)
Cumberland Presbyterian Doctrine
Cumberland Presbyterian History
The Cumberland Presbyterian Church at Work
Teaching in the Church

Or a miniseries over a period of time on:

How to make a visit in hospital and home
How to work with youth
How to work with children
How to work with older people
How to help others

Any innovations should be decided upon not only by pastor and elders, but by the entire congregation. The suggestions which we have just made may not seem to be innovative. Many churches have done these things. However, there are others for whom they are ideas which have never been tried.

Pastors and elders are primary administrators (orchestrators) of Christian Education. They are responsible for putting it all together and making the music of learning and spiritual growth. A guide to good administration is to center it on people, not organization or program. When we center it on people, and not organization, we ask, How can we help children, youth and adults move from stage to stage in their journey of faith?

How can we cut down on duplication of effort often found in the church?
How can we set up classes and groups which are dynamic and effective in serving people's needs?
Do we have organizations or groups which no longer serve a need? What new groups need to be organized?
Do our leaders, literature, and space serve the needs of people?

When we put people in the center of our attention, there is a vision of Christian education which otherwise is missing.

The pastor and elders cannot escape their role as administrators. They either do it, or see that someone else does it properly, and in accordance with their best insights and knowledge.

Pastors and elders are evaluators. We are to ask, How well are we doing in helping the people move forward from stage to stage in their Christian growth? There are ways of doing this and resources for doing it. The *Christian Education Plan Book* contains resources for evaluation and to aid in carrying forward other

---

[18] See *Smaller Church Mission Study Guide,* Henry A. Blunk, Geneva Press, 1978, or order materials from Board of Missions, 1978 Union, Memphis, TN 38104.

ideas already mentioned. See also a very fine resource under note 19 below

MOTIVATION

Perhaps, as we have considered the task of Christian Education and the role of the pastor as a teacher and educator, we have come to feel that we pastors have much more than we can do. We have considered the scope of the ministry into which we have been called. We have examined the call and its meaning. We have examined the offers and demands of ordination. We have studied our roles as pastor, leader of worship, and preacher. We have now just completed a overview of our duties as teacher and educator. The demands of ministry seem to grow beyond our ability to comprehend and execute. We may be pondering how we can do it, not only in reference to time, but also to ability and strength. Further, upon looking at the task of Christian Education, we may wonder how we can move the church toward a truly effective program of Christian nurture. Will it respond? Will the elders cooperate?

We will give some thoughts now to motivation for the task of Christian Education both for the pastor and the people. Also, we hope it will provide encouragement and motivation for the ministry in general, especially for pastors. How can we keep going in view of the many dimensions of ministry? What resources will give us the power to overcome our problems and limitations? How can we reach our possibilities? How can we face and overcome despair and drift?

We are called and sent. We were not enlisted by human beings. God is behind our call and commitment. This moves us to feel deeply about our mission, and gives strength and hope as we face the future. Sometimes the call will hold us to the path when nothing else will.

There is an urgency for teaching on every age level. People grow and change rapidly. Opportunity for teaching individuals, especially children and youth, can pass us by in a hurry unless we take advantage of it. Needs on one developmental level must be filled before others on higher levels can be taken care of. If the foundation is not laid from stage to stage, next steps cannot be taken. Unless we teach we can lose the Christian faith, for we are always just one generation from the extinction of Christianity.

But beyond children and youth, enormous needs for continued growth arise in middle and later adulthood for helping meet the demands and carrying the burdens of maturity. Most of the problems which arise in the church are due to the fact that adults stopped growing. Further, in recent years we have discovered that there are needs and possibilities for growth and development even in old age and no one can reach fulfillment unless these are met. Hence, the Third Age Ministry which was initiated in 1990.

There is a pressing need for assistance in living the Christian life in a pluralistic and changing society. Our negligence is often dramatically evident when we see our children and youth drawn to strange sects and religious cults, or to no faith at all. These crises shock us deeply and open our eyes to the critical importance of teaching. It has always been difficult to educate for living and

---

[19] See *Christian Education in the Small Church*, Griggs and Walther, Judson Press, Pages 39-47 for roles of educational leaders.

mission in the world. It is more arduous now. Loss of traditional values in our culture, disruption in family life, new and strange religious movements, emphasis on sex and things, mobility, and growing population, all combine to challenge us to teach well.

We are encouraged when we recognize that people are learning in community. Growth and change occur in people beyond the planned program of Christian nurture. It is probably true that they learn more from family relations, worship, fellowship, service, the sacraments, mission, and preaching, than in any other ways. There is more than meets the eye in every situation. The whole church teaches. But this is not an invitation to be careless in planning and administering a formal program of Christian teaching. In some cases people learn the wrong things; and many families are not teaching anything positive and often teach the wrong things. Nevertheless, many families are making an effort to rear their children as Christians and to support each other in their faith. They need the help of the church, hence the need for more family education.

The conviction that the gospel fills the basic needs of people is a strong motivator. To believe there is nothing in the world to match it is to preach and teach it with fervor. We believe it speaks to our basic needs for assurance, acceptance, love, hope, purpose and challenge in life. It is the Word of Life. This Word of reconciliation has been entrusted to our hands and we must treat it carefully. The gospel is the touchstone by which we test values. The touchstone was a type of black stone formerly used to test the purity of silver and gold by the streak it left on it when it was rubbed with the metal. It has come to mean any test or criterion for determining genuineness or value. In this day of confused values, we need such a standard. The gospel provides it. The gospel also says Christ is the bread, water, light, life and salt of existence. Teachers and preachers are mediators of this good news.

The faith that God works in the process of change and growth is our greatest encouragement. "If God be for us who can be against us?" The Holy Spirit initiates

---

FOR FURTHER CONSIDERATION

❖ Can you willingly accept your role as teacher-educator as outlined in this chapter?

❖ Do you believe you have potential as a teacher? Are you willing to learn?

❖ Do you believe Christian education is as important as the chapter has affirmed?

❖ Are you willing to accept the responsibilities outlined for pastors and elders?

❖ Do you see yourself as being responsible for leading and teaching the elders?

❖ Have the ideas presented above given you a challenge and engendered some excitement concerning the possibilities for the growth of persons and your role in encouraging it? Are you willing to accept your role as a model in Christian growth?

❖ When you observe any person in any stage of life, do you try to imagine what they can become through Christ in your ministry?

❖ Are you definitely motivated to your task?

❖ Are you willing to read and study some of the resources listed at left, especially the first few?

and sustains the process of growth in us. It is not our program, but God's. We work with him. God is carrying it in and through the church. God is the source of grace and the urge toward development and maturity. It is for us to find out where and in whom the Holy Spirit is working and to work cooperatively.

> I planted, Apollos watered, but God gave the growth. So neither the one who plants nor the one who waters is anything, but only God who gives the growth. The one who plants and the one who waters have a common purpose, and each will receive wages according to the labor of each. For we are God's servants, working together; you are God's field, God's building.[20]

Doubtless, there are many, many more things to be said about the pastor as a teacher-educator. There is yet much more for us to learn. It is hoped that this chapter will have given a brief but adequate overview of our role as Christian educators, and at least some motivation for filling it and learning more about how to serve in this channel, whether we are beginners or veterans.

FOR FURTHER READING AND STUDY

Christian Education in the Small Church, Griggs and Walther, Judson Press, 1988.

Christian Education Plan Book, Federated Board of Christian Education, CP Church

Third Age Ministry In the Congregation, Federated Board of Christian Education, Cumberland Presbyterian Church, 1990.

Journey of Faith, Pepper and Wood, Board of Christian Education, Cumberland Presbyterian Church, 1985, a recommended resource for communicants' classes.

Teaching in the Community of Faith, Charles R. Foster, Abingdon, 1982.

The Big Little School, 200 Years of the Sunday School, Lynn and Wright, Abingdon, 1971.

Where Faith Begins, C. Ellis Nelson, John Knox Press, 1967.

The Missionary Messenger and

The Cumberland Presbyterian—These periodicals carry articles pertaining to the whole ministry of the church, including Christian Education. For example: "The Awkward Years," Tom Gillis and Lori Gillis, *The Cumberland Presbyterian,* issue of April 1990, and "The Lord is My Teacher, I Shall Not Fail" by retiring Moderator Beverly St.John, issue of June 15, 1989.

---

[20] I Corinthians 3:6-9 NRSV

CHAPTER 8
The Pastor As Evangelist

A BASIC ASSUMPTION

This chapter is written on the assumption that evangelism is to be done by and through the whole church, with the pastor taking the lead. Further, evangelism is to communicate the whole gospel to the whole person—all the person's relationships and all areas of that person's life. We are not engaged in saving souls anymore than Jesus was. Our aim is to save lives. The words we use—save, redeem, reconcile—indicate that we are attempting to bring people into a relationship with God, with self and with others in which love is the main principle.

Although the pastor will take the lead in doing, training and involving others in the work of evangelism, the pastor cannot do it all. Nor can the pastor be expected to succeed unless the whole church is supportive and cooperative. The entire church, as a fellowship and as individual members, will contribute to or take from the effectiveness of evangelistic ventures. The spirit of the congregation, the degree of its commitment, the quality of its love, the extent of its warmth and hospitality contribute to the outcome of its outreach.

This concept of evangelism is given support by Dr. Wayne Oates, author, counselor, and professor of psychiatry and behavioral sciences. He quotes Samuel Southard who defines pastoral evangelism as the

> dialogue in which the Christian's actions and attitudes of loving care and righteous discipline, empowered by the Holy Spirit, awaken a non-Christian so that he will receive Christ as divine Savior and Lord of his life in the Christian fellowship and in the world.

Dr. Oates makes this comment about the definition:

> This understanding of evangelism contrasts "instant evangelism" with the "pastoral patience" that takes into consideration the total pilgrimage of the person, his history of encounter with sin and grace, his family context, his vocational meaning in life, and the durable relationships he builds with the fellowship of believers of whom the pastor is one significant representative.

> Southard insists that the convert needs an adequate interpretation of his experience, recognition, and acceptance by Christian people who become genuinely important to him, and personal unburdening of the weights and sins that hinder him as lively memories prior to his decision to be Christian. The pastoral evangelist moves with the individual away from isolation to intimacy in the small-group fellowship of the church and enables the person to participate according to his abilities and station in life with persons who value him for his own sake and not for what he can "do" for the organization of the church.[1]

What has just been said needs to be pondered. It may appear to be heavy stuff with which we are being confronted at the outset of this chapter. However, these quotations embody the basic understanding of the meaning of evangelism which we wish to emphasize.

EVANGELISM IN THE WORLD AS IT IS

Before we go further in discussing the meaning of evangelism, we need to recognize some things about the world in which it is done, and how this affects our approach.

The evangelistic outreach of the disciples and apostles was affected by the nature of their times. Jesus lived and completed his mission in a more or less simple agricultural society. Palestine was a small country under Roman rule. The people thought, felt and reacted in ways that were natural to their environment and traditions. Jesus and the disciples used methods of outreach which were appropriate to their situation.

When Christians were driven out of Jerusalem and moved into a larger world they had to adapt their approaches. Some of their conflicts were over ways they could adjust to new situations and cultures. A reading of Acts will inform us about the methods they used in evangelism.

The same thing is true of us today. The kind of evangelism our fathers and forefathers did will hardly apply today. We have to take into account the changes which have occurred even in the last few years in life styles, attitudes, beliefs and practices. We do not mean we must compromise our message. It is the same. But the approaches we make in communicating it must be modified. Perhaps a few quotes will illustrate what is being said.

Some of us can remember when the society of which we were a part supported our religious beliefs. A great deal of Christianity had been instilled into the culture. This is not as true now.

> Protestant Christianity in America has historically relied upon its societal environment for the reinforcement of its theological convictions and its moral commitments. This reliance has been focused particularly upon public education. The sociologists note, however, that our social and cultural environment has changed dramatically in this second half of the 20th century, making our reliance upon that environment for support of our Christian vision of life mere wishful thinking.

---

[1] *The Christian Pastor*, Wayne E. Oates, Westminster, 1964, pages 18, 19

> Such reinforcement, in point of fact, is simply no longer there. What is there amounts to a groundswell of skepticism in regard to the truth claims made by religions in general and Christianity in particular.[2]
>
> The Christian faith and the life of discipleship today are counter-cultural commitments that we must do everything within our power to encourage and reinforce among the young and old.[3]
>
> It is not so often acknowledged that evangelism means calling people to believe something which is radically different from what is normally accepted as public truth, and that it calls for a conversion not only of the heart and will but of the mind. A serious commitment to evangelism, to the telling of the story which the Church is sent to tell, means a radical questioning of the reigning assumptions of public life. It is to affirm the gospel not only as an invitation to private and personal decision but as public truth which ought to be acknowledged as true for the whole of life of society.[4]

One of the big problems of evangelism today is related to what has been said about the reigning assumptions of public life. How can the church call people to make such a commitment when so many of its members live by those very assumptions and whose religion is a compromised Christianity? If we are to be effective there must be credibility in our words and professions. There must be a reason for others to believe the evangelistic witness we offer. That is why it is so important for the church to think first of all about its witness to the world. *Credibility is a base for evangelism.*

Further, in view of the fact that people have become more secularized, we will have to do some unlearning of the old and learning of the new approaches to evangelism. People think differently from the way they did even a few years ago, and we have to change our strategy. New books and articles are being written to guide us.[5]

THE NATURE OF EVANGELISM

A strange phenomenon is that in spite of our faith and experience, our theology, all our talk, and the plethora of evangelistic efforts, we find evangelism difficult to define. We are not sure if a definition can catch and express its meaning, depth and scope. Maybe the truest definition is that *evangelism is simply introducing people to Jesus Christ in all the ways we know how, and bringing them into the fellowship of the church.*

The Reverend William G. Enright, in an article in the *Presbyterian Outlook* a few years ago, says, after describing an innovative program in his congregation, that *evangelism is a result.* "Evangelism takes place where the Spirit is at work

---

[2] *The Presbyterian Outlook*, July 18-25, 1988, "The Way Back Leads Nowhere" Thomas W. Gillespie

[3] *The Presbyterian Outlook*, February 27, 1989, "Let's Smash an Idol" Lionel R. Lindsay

[4] *Truth to Tell: The Gospel as Public Truth*, Lesslie Newbigin, Eerdmans, 1991, page 2

[5] *How to Reach Secular People*, George Hunter, Abingdon, 1992 and
Missionary Messenger, September 1991, "Growth and Pastoral Visitation," Jack Barker

through people. Evangelism is good news for all people, for the whole man. As people are touched by the love of God where they are and as the gospel comes alive for them in new ways they seek out the source of that love and new insight."

This is a valuable insight. This often happens when we have invited and helped someone to relate to our congregation. Becoming a part of and sharing in the fellowship and getting involved in the church's life, and being warmed in the Spirit, the person often begins to ask questions and to seek answers. Clark Williamson, pioneer educator in our church, once said, "You can open an egg in two ways. You can crack it on the skillet, or you can warm it and let is hatch." *Maybe evangelism is warming people to the point that a new birth occurs, a new life is hatched.* It takes a little time and is never instantaneous.

Several years ago we wrote to Dudley Condron, editor of *The Missionary Messenger*, requesting a listing of books on evangelism and asking if he had something to share about the subject and its meaning. This is what he wrote:

> Today Christian Education and Evangelism are meeting at the point of worship/celebration. People who feel loved and accepted of God, accept one another, or want to listen to one another's hurts, really hear one another, feel heard too, come to know what it means to be a channel of grace, peace and love. They have something to celebrate, and will worship. *In that remarkable setting evangelism gets done. No technique to it—it just happens sometimes,* and we celebrate that too.

People who try to make evangelism into methods and techniques miss the mark. There is a place, however, for the use of various means of evangelism, if they blend with the entire spiritual process of intercommunication.

What do you think about the concepts of evangelism which follow?

> *Evangelism isn't a program; it's a miracle.* When a person comes to believe that the story of a Jew executed by the state 2,000 years ago has everything to do with his life as a 20th century American, when he [or she] believes that story is also his or her story, that's evangelism!...
>
> True evangelism is what Jesus did the day he decided to have lunch with Zaccheus...
>
> Evangelism happens more by serendipity than by design... Occasionally, evangelism happens in my church, but again it is serendipitous, a gift of that wildly independent Holy Spirit who insists on blowing wherever it will without taking orders from me...
>
> Can we be honest enough and humble enough simply to say to people, "We need you. We have found joy, strength and hope for our spirits and our lives in the Christian faith and in this congregation in particular. Maybe you will, too. Would you be willing to find out?" We need not be embarrassed by such appeals.[6]

---

[6] *The Presbyterian Outlook*, a 1985 edition, "True Evangelism" Patricia Lovelace

BIBLICAL MODELS OF EVANGELISM

Andrew is a good model of personal evangelism. See John 1:40-43. When Andrew met Jesus, the very first thing he did was to go to his brother Simon, and to say, "We have found the Christ." Then he brought him and introduced him to Jesus. That is evangelism. It happens in a hundred ways and there is no one particular pattern. There is only the deep desire to introduce others to Jesus Christ because of what he can do for them.

Philip is another model from whom we can learn. Read Acts 8:26-40. Here is what the incident of Philip's evangelizing the Eunuch says to us.

First, he was sent to the desert road by the Holy Spirit. In fact, the Holy Spirit is the chief actor, not Philip or the Eunuch. God is the true evangelist who seeks every person.

> God acted redemptively in Jesus Christ because of the sins of the world and continues with the same intent in the Holy Spirit to call every person to repentance and faith.[7]

We who do evangelism are not initiators. We only work with God who is always first on the scene. This is a strengthening, and humbling, fact to remember.

Second, Philip had knowledge and experience of Christ and the scriptures from which to draw as he guided the Ethiopian. This is essential to evangelism. He was a true believer who knew enough to be able to talk about faith. He had struggled with his own growth and development. He knew what it was to have questions and doubts, and he did not take lightly the matter of being a Christian. This enabled him to understand something of the process through which the other person was going.

Third, Philip was ready when this unexpected opportunity arose. Although we tend to do evangelism by plan, God prepares often to send us unexpected opportunities to communicate the gospel. These may be the best openings we ever have. Some readiness is already there, and readiness is one of the laws of learning. Philip in response to this readiness, was able to speak from his own knowledge in a natural and spontaneous way, out of his preparedness.

Fourth, Most, if not all of us, need help in coming to Christ. The man asked, "How can I unless someone guides me?" when Philip asked if he understood what he was reading. There are many who are wanting someone to come and help them. Our offer of help is not an intrusion on them, but a welcomed assistance. We can supply information, share thoughts, make suggestions, give encouragement, and relax them so they will know they can respond openly and honestly. It is always important to enable people to respond without fear of rejection or judgment, to ask questions and even to voice doubts.

Fifth, Philip answered questions when they were asked, and not before. Learning takes place when questions indicate a desire to know. Too often we try to give answers before questions are asked, and so they are ignored. What are the questions in the minds and hearts of people? These are our cues. We may also prompt questions to be asked and thus arouse interest.

---

[7] *Confession of Faith*, 4.01, page 7

There are other biblical models of evangelism. Jesus sent the twelve disciples out to do visitation.[8] At another time he sent out the seventy.[9]

Acts records the coming of the Holy Spirit and Peter's subsequent sermon to thousands.[10] Other passages record further incidents of mass evangelism.

Acts also tells of Paul's stay in Ephesus, during which he held discussions and did what might be called educational evangelism.[11] Other passages in Acts tell of various methods by which the gospel was communicated.

HOW ONE CHURCH GREW AND WHY

We have been dealing with ideas and concepts up to this point. Now we want to turn to more practical matters and see how these theories work out in practice. We have chosen a congregation which illustrates what has been discussed. The pastor has been on the field for eighteen years. The church has grown slowly in numbers, spirit, service and stewardship during this period. It is located in a county seat town of 15,000 population, which has increased in size, also.

The pastor says the church has grown in spite of the lack of effort to make it grow. He means by this that they have no special organization to foster growth. They do not do visitation on an organized basis, other than what is done largely by the pastor and a few others who make occasional visits. There is a great desire to bring new people into its fellowship, but a great reluctance to do anything which seems to be contrived, superficial or manipulative. Part of this is due to the nature of the people of the area, and part by design.

The philosophy which seems to direct them is this. They try to find needs of people and to minister to them in the spirit of Christ. As they minister to people some of them become a part of the fellowship of the church, and finally covenant members. They, in turn, become a part of the ministering congregation.

They are concerned that they grow numerically, for they gain and lose members at about the normal rate. However, they are concerned that they minister to people, and that they work in such a way as to foster the deepest and most permanent kind of commitment and quality of Christian experience. They do not believe the burden of church growth rests on their shoulders but on God, the real evangelist, who calls people into the church. It is their task to learn to work with God and be worked through by God.

Here is a statement about the church which the pastor made when he was asked to write a brief paper on the work and growth of his congregation. He notes twelve (12) items.

1. We are in a county seat town of about 15,000 population which has grown slowly and somewhat spasmodically over the past several years. Because of the size of the community and nature of the congregation we are fairly visible to everyone.
2. We are the only Presbyterian Church in town that offers a resident pastor and a full program. We have adequate building facilities.

---

[8] Matthew 10:5-15; Mark 6:7-13; Luke 9:1-6

[9] Luke 10:1-12

[10] Acts 2

[11] Acts 19

3. Our worship is orderly, but warm and spiritual (we would like to think). It is neither highly liturgical nor extremely informal.
4. We use a low key, cultivative approach to evangelism which seems to be much more effective than the more "pushy" type used by some groups in our community. We are willing to wait for people to make up their own minds in coming to a decision.
5. We try to keep the primary emphasis on persons rather than the institution without neglecting the institution.
6. Our church is said (by some) to be warm and friendly to people who come to worship.
7. The pastor makes a lot of visits and tries to cultivate a relationship before attempting to talk about church membership.
8. We have many friends in the community who alert us to new families who move to the community whom they feel may be interested in our particular congregation.
9. We try to be a caring church and have some established means of expressing it.
10. The pastor and many of the people are active in the community and are seen as being interested in the total life of the community.
11. We try to minister to the needs of groups, like youth, young adults, children, and older adults.
12. Our church grows in spite of the lack of effort to make it grow. I doubt seriously if the major purpose in all we do is church growth. I like to think it is to minister. Because of this we look constantly for ways we can organize to serve more acceptably.

So much for what the pastor says. Questions concerning why the church grew were asked a number of the church members. Here is a composite of their answers.

1. We offer a variety of opportunities to fill the variety of needs in the congregation.
2. Members accept each other as they are and where they are in their Christian development.
3. We offer good programs for children and youth.
4. We seem to be like a family.
5. Young adults have developed some strong relationships and have become a good supportive group. This has been the source of a lot of good influence and useful service to others.
6. We have been stimulated by new leadership which has attracted more people.

How would we evaluate this church? First, we must remember that it is only one congregation in one situation and is not representative of all congregations. So it is not a model for everyone. However, it has some basic points which suggest one way in which evangelism and growth can be achieved. There are also some basic principles at work here which can apply to every situation.

It does not appear to be a congregation which has approached perfection. It is not what you would call a "complete" church by any means. It has enough of the average and ordinary about it that we do not feel threatened by it. Yet, it says some good things to us and indicates that there are more than one way to do evangelism and achieve church growth.

What are some of the things about it that impress us and which suggest ways we may improve our congregations? How about these?

> A growing community enables the church to grow.
> The church has made itself visible. The people know it is there.
> Spiritual worship.
> Low key approach to evangelism.
> Centers its ministry on persons.
> The pastor visits and cultivates relationships.
> Growth is incidental to ministry.
> It is like a family.
> It ministers to various groups.

CONGREGATIONS WHICH ARE EFFECTIVE IN EVANGELISM

Congregations which are effective in evangelism reflect certain characteristics.

- They do not use a single, simple approach, but *use many means and methods*.
- They do *not leave the responsibility altogether to the pastor*. Congregations which do this do not reach many people outside the church.
- *Training in evangelism* makes a great difference in effectiveness.
- They are *friendly* toward strangers, newcomers and outsiders.
- Evangelism is not something added, but is a *part of the total mission and ministry* of the church.
- They *think of themselves as a mission*, rather than a fellowship of the redeemed. Too many churches are ghettos in which the members isolate themselves from the world.
- They have *learned how to communicate* with people of our secular society. Often we only talk to ourselves and do not know how to talk to people outside the faith.
- They have come to *expect a great deal from their members*, and are not afraid to enlist them in action.
- They *invite people to come to church*. This is so important we want to give a special emphasis to it.

> Lutheran church historian Martin Marty says that one word defines the difference between churches that grow and those that don't: *Invite!* Marty reports a study that indicates that the average [Here he names a member of a certain denomination] invites someone to church once every 28 years. His statistic may be exaggerated, but his point is not. When a church isn't growing its members are not "inviting."
>
> A study of new members who joined the Christian Church (Disciples) says that 77.6% attended the first time because of "relational influences": they heard about the church through a friend, acquaintance or relative. This confirms the maxim of the Institute of American Church Growth in Pasadena, California: 70-90% of the persons who join any church come through the influence of a friend, acquaintance or relative. No amount of pulpit power can overcome a lack of individual invitational expression from the pews.[12]

---

[12] *How to Build a Magnetic Church*, Herb Miller, Abingdon, 143 pages, paperback, 1991

A WORKABLE PLAN OF EVANGELISM

We have discussed the nature of evangelism and how the whole church is involved. We have indicated the difficulty of doing evangelism in a secular world. We have shared some biblical models. We moved on then to discuss church growth and the characteristics of congregations that grow. There is much more that needs to be said but this chapter is to be largely an introduction to church growth and evangelism. It cannot give much on techniques and skills in pastoral evangelism. This can come later.

Perhaps the most helpful thing will be to propose what can be considered a workable plan of evangelism, one which can be done in any church anywhere. Too often we grow discouraged because the task seems too big and complicated. Hence, we are outlining a brief, simple, but inclusive five-point plan as a guide for you to follow in your work as pastor in the field of evangelism.

1. *Visitation*. Visit persons who are possible candidates for conversion and/or church membership. Enlist lay persons of the church to visit with you. New people moving into a community make better candidates than those who have lived a long time in a community but have never committed themselves. However, no one should be neglected. We never know when changes may occur in people making them susceptible to the gospel.

Do not be overly aggressive during these visits. Cultivate relationships with people and move naturally from one stage to another, when you may be able to discuss religion with them. Build bridges into their lives. Be interested in them as people, not mere "prospects" for building an institution. Be interested in their total lives. Remember you are a pastor. Listen more than you talk. Ask questions. Listen for their hurts, feelings, needs, experiences, problems, doubts and questions. Don't argue. Keep the door of their minds open.

Of course, there really are no set rules to follow. Be led by the Spirit, common sense, and love. We have to feel our way along with people knowing that each person and family is different. Visit! Make contact. Get out into the world and out of the ghetto. You don't save the world outside by staying inside.

2. *Invitation*. Get your people to follow your lead in inviting people to the church. Ask them to invite their neighbors and friends, and those whom they meet socially and where they work. Offer to pick people up and bring them with you. The importance of invitations has already been stressed. This is the best evangelism you can do. It is simple. It does not require a lot of baggage. It is natural. It requires only a few words and no big speeches. You don't have to be a professional to do it.

3. *Education*. This is done by teachers of youth, children and adults. With children no pressure is to be applied, but interpretations of the meaning of being a Christian , with gentle suggestions to respond when the times seems ripe. This can be done in classes of youth and adults who are willing to sign up for a communicant's class. *Journey of Faith* is a good resource. Day camps, Vacation Church School, camps and other group meetings provide further opportunity for educational evangelism. As has already been mentioned, the pastor has many and varied chances to teach as he comes and goes among the people.

4. *Proclamation*. Preach gospel sermons with the offer of salvation and the

call to service and obedience. Give invitations.

Preach pastoral sermons to meet people's needs, with the knowledge that these can also be evangelistic. When our messages meet the needs of people we are appealing also to the interests of those who might not have become Christian. They hear what Christ can do for and to them.

Hold a high standard of commitment to and service for Jesus Christ. Challenge people to leave their selfishness to care for others in His name. There are benefits in becoming a Christian but these should be secondary to the higher motives of doing the difficult and courageous. Call on people to love in a cold world, to care in a cruel one, to believe in a sceptical one and to give themselves away in the name of Christ, with little emphasis on the benefits and blessings. Appeal to strengths, not weaknesses. Arouse the unconsenting conscience. People, whether they know it or not, are waiting for a message that will call forth their very best, and ask a great deal of them. We are not trying to enlist weaklings.

5. *Congregation.* Let us say it again. The life of the congregation contributes to or takes from effective evangelism. If the congregation is made up of warm, believing, witnessing, loving members who are trying to grow in grace and who take their faith seriously, it will make an impact upon those who grow up in its midst and those who observe it from the outside. The spiritual quality of the congregation is an evangelistic force.

This chapter is only a beginning. Think of it as a springboard from which you can dive deeply into the refreshing and renewing waters of evangelism.

How shall they believe in him of whom they have not heard?

> How beautiful are the feet of them that preach the gospel of peace, and bring glad tidings of good things![13]

FOR FURTHER CONSIDERATION

- How would you define evangelism?
- Do you agree that we need new ways of doing evangelism?
- How can you lead your people into learning how to reach secular people?
- Do you agree or disagree?
  ___ Evangelism is not a program but a miracle?
  ___ Evangelism is a result?
  ___ Inviting people to church is highly effective in evangelism.
- What factors do you see in your church which make for growth and evangelism?
- Will the simple program for evangelism on pages (98-99) work in your church?

---

[13] Romans 10:14, 15 KJV

FOR FURTHER READING AND STUDY

Truth to Tell: The Gospel and Public Truth, Lesslie Newbigin, Eerdmans, 1991
How to Reach Secular People, George Hunter, Abingdon, 1992
How to Build a Magnetic Church, Herb Miller, Abingdon, paperback, 1991.

Two books will be helpful in learning more about doing evangelism in a small church. They are:

Making the Small Church Effective, Carl S. Dudley, Abingdon, 1978. Read especially, Chapter 3, "Growth by Adoption" pages 46-60.

Developing Your Small Church's Potential, Dudley and Walrath, Judson Press, 1988. Read especially Chapter 3 "Integrating Community Change into the Small Church," pages 50-76, which gives you an approach to growth and evangelism and how to integrate new members into the congregation.

Write the Cumberland Presbyterian Board of Missions for leaflets, pamphlets, and recommended books. This will bring you into contact with the most current materials on evangelism and church growth.

Subscribe to *The Missionary Messenger* and *The Cumberland Presbyterian* and keep alert to articles which pertain to missions and evangelism. For example: "Being Witness" *Cumberland Presbyterian,* issue of November 1990, and "Arrows: Defending the Native American life-world with stories that have a point," Robert N. Bellah, issue of November 1, 1989. Read *Missionary Messenger,* issue on Evangelism, February 1992. Excellent.

CHAPTER 9

The Pastor as Administrator

In addition to other roles, the pastor serves as administrator of the church program. This function is biblical. "And God has appointed in the church first apostles, second prophets, third teachers, then workers of miracles, then leaders, helpers, *administrators,* speakers in various kinds of tongues.[1] The New Revised Standard Version translates "administrators" as "forms of leadership." In this role the pastor manages the affairs of the church.

Most ministers tend to put administration at the bottom of the scale in importance and enjoyment. They react to the matter-of-factness of the task. They prefer to be engaged in more inspirational matters. It involves so many details that use valuable time. However, it is a job we cannot escape. Providing guidance and giving direction to the church are expected of us.

Here is an interesting fact. Research has shown that although ministers may give administration a low score, the average minister will spend one-half of his or her time with it! Whether we want it or not, sooner or later the administrative role will push itself on us. Regardless of whether we like it or not, it is important for it deals with the *total ministry* of the church and *ties everything together.*

Anything that affects the life of the church is a concern of the pastor. The minister is an overseer and has oversight of the entire congregation. Various translations of Acts 20:28 refer to pastors and elders as overseers, guardians, and shepherds of "*all* the flock." *All* is an inclusive word. No person or persons, no group or groups, can claim to be free of the oversight of the pastor and elders.

The pastor is *the* leader, *not just one* of the leaders. This does not mean pastors ought to be autocratic. They are shepherds. Democratic leadership characterizes their role. But they *do* lead. "If the trumpet give an uncertain sound, who shall prepare himself to the battle?"[2]

---

[1] I Corinthians 12:28

[2] I Corinthians 14:8 KJV

Pastor administrators share leadership with elders and other leaders. Shared leadership proves to be most effective and acceptable. We work *with* and not *for* people, and not *instead* of them. Remember Moses. As a young man he wanted to do something *for* the Hebrews. In trying to do so, he killed an Egyptian and had to leave the country. He had lost his opportunity. Later, when God called him back he learned to work *with* others. Aaron and Miriam became his aides, and Jethro, his father-in-law taught him how to share his responsibilities as judge of the people.[3] Our system of government provides for shared leadership between pastors and people.[4]

Before we go further, let us take a look at the meaning and purpose of administration. *Administration means providing guidance so that good things can happen.* It includes leading, planning, organizing, coordinating and administering. It also has to do with methods, with the how of getting things done. How something is done can be as important as what is being done. *How* and *what* are like *husband* and *wife*. They blend together. Important things in the church do not just happen. They are made to happen. They must be moved and guided.

To save administration from being a routine, uninteresting duty we reluctantly perform, let it center in persons. Its purpose is to make possible ministry to, for, by and with the parishioners. In this way it becomes personal and not mechanical. We are working with warm, feeling, changing, growing, living souls, not just plans, ideas and organizations.

To illustrate, think of administering a program of evangelism. Why are you doing it? Do you wish to help the church grow in numbers, or are you wanting to introduce Bill, Mary, Joe or Jim to Jesus Christ and bring them into full membership of the church? In doing Christian education are you just wanting the Sunday school to grow, or are you wanting to help fourth grader Ellen, and teenager Scott, or adult Arlene, or third ager Richard take the next step they are ready to take in spiritual growth? Thinking of persons makes all the difference!

Administration has to do with *planning*. The amount of planning is determined by the size and nature of the congregation. It can include setting goals for the year; organizing for a new year in Christian education; initiating a fellowship program; getting ready for a revival; enlisting people to do visitation; doing repairs on the church building; seeking more space for group meetings; getting ready to observe Advent and Christmas and/or Lent and Easter; setting up a library and so on.

Administration has to do with *organizing*. This may include the initiation of a rotation system for elders and deacons; nominating and electing officials; setting up committees of worship, Christian Education, Missions, Finance and others; beginning new Sunday school classes; selecting and enlisting leaders and other items.

Administration has to do with *coordinating*. Coordination is for the purpose of preventing overlapping of activities, preventing conflicts in meeting places and dates, encouraging cooperation, and enabling the church to move together as a unit.

---

[3] Exodus 18:13-24

[4] See *The First Parish*, Cook, Abingdon, pages 25-27, on good leadership styles and qualities.

To achieve this a church calendar may be prepared and displayed for information on dates of meetings and activities; a person or committee may work with the pastor in clearinghouse duties; the church news letter may carry announcements of all programs. Nothing should be planned without clearing with all persons and groups involved. This prevents the church from moving in many directions and having groups bump into each other. It also saves hurt feelings and broken relations. Many problems can be prevented by good coordination.

Administration has to do with *administering,* or getting the job done. Someone or some group must be responsible for moving things along. It is essential that an understanding of who is responsible for what is agreed upon.

Administering will include such things as the following: meeting with committees; seeing that they do what has been planned; hearing reports; carrying out plans by assigning responsibilities to the proper committees; working with the session, Sunday school officers and teachers; delegating responsibilities; evaluating what is being done; and probably many other actions.

At this point, you may be wondering where to start in this work of administration. When you become pastor of a church you assume responsibility for administration. You find in that particular church a program which has been established and in operation for some time. It may or may not be to your liking, but you have inherited it. It probably has been accepted by the members. You may see things immediately which you would like to change. You may want to introduce some new ideas. If you are wise, you will exercise patience and give yourselves time to understand the situation, to learn how the people feel, what their relations are, and who the leaders are before you initiate changes.

Good administrators keep one big thing in mind. The program of the church belongs to the people. If it is their program they will support it. If it is the pastor's program they may not, or they may accept it without much enthusiasm. In view of this, we enlist their participation when we begin to plan for something new. With them, we will determine if it is needed, set goals, establish priorities, define steps to be taken, and assign responsibilities.

Good administrators do not spring new ideas on the session or other groups "out of the blue," in spite of how great those ideas seem to be. They learn that many plans are rejected simply because the people were not prepared to consider them. Timing is of the essence in getting new plans accepted.

Good administrators do not get too much in a hurry, nor do they push hard for their proposals. They give the people time to think and to respond. Many meetings may be held before final adoption.

Good administrators do not think they are always right or have all the good concepts. They seek advice and information from others. They believe there are good resources in any group and that often the ideas of lay persons are better than the pastor's. Some of us have become convinced that there are adequate resources in any group to carry out the plan or program the group creates.

Good administrators think thoroughly through what they want to propose. They write down, read over and over, and evaluate carefully the plans they are developing. They are willing to encourage questions and objections, and to explain and explain. They are willing to get key persons to evaluate their suggestions.

Good administrators tell what they want and why, what will be required and what the plan may cost. They work out all possible details.

Good administrators are able to accept failure without letting their feelings get hurt, or without getting angry. They refuse to let failure drive wedges of division between them and others. They live to try another day. They are able to realize that the people may not be ready to approve a proposal. They do not allow abortive attempts to discourage them from dreaming.

Good administrators know that frequent evaluation of the church's program is essential to its health and improvement. They involve others in the use of evaluative methods without hesitation. They do not let some programs acquire a halo of sanctity. They do not want programs for the sake of programs, lest the church become a bureaucracy. They learn to turn loose and let go of even their most cherished plan if it is not meeting needs.

Good administrators recognize the dire need for the work of the church to be coordinated to prevent conflict and overlapping. They engage every means and all necessary persons to help them do it.

Perhaps *models of different sizes and types of churches* may further enlighten our understanding of administration. We will give two. They are actual churches but their names and names of pastors are withheld.

The first one will be called Evergreen. It is a small church in a small community with a history of strength in numbers and influence beginning in the 1800s. Like other rural churches it has lost members because of the shift of population and now has only about twenty (20) members. It has services only twice a month. It thinks as much about survival as service and wonders how long it can continue. It has three elders, two of whom are women. It continues with a very limited Sunday school, only for adults. It has an occasional fellowship meal and has until recently celebrated Christmas with a great emphasis on children of the community. It holds an annual revival. The remaining members are loyal and manifest a high quality of churchmanship.

We will describe some of the things done by a pastor who served for a period of four years. He lived elsewhere but visited regularly in the community and was interested in the welfare of the community. After a few months he outlined a few things he would like to see the church accomplish. It being a small church, administration was fairly simple and was done more or less informally.

He preached a sermon one Sunday on helping the church to make advances. He met with the session afterward and outlined his proposals. They voted to accept them. He than took them to the congregation and explained them, having provided copies for each person. Some of his ideas were dropped and others added. The people seemed to appreciate what he was doing, but they also felt free to say what they thought might work, and what might not, and to allow him a chance to try with alternate plans.

The program he suggested, after being revised by the session and congregation, included such things as:

    A request that elders give full support to church and Sunday school
    A request that the congregation do the same
    A proposed understanding about finances
    An agreement that the church would be represented at presbytery and synod
    A statement of appreciation that the church supported OUO and presbyterial and synodic budgets
    A request that filmstrips and other means be used to acquaint the church with

the entire CP program. A suggestion to visit the Birthplace near Dickson.
Distribution of missions leaflets monthly
Effort to reach out through visitation
Setting up a service fund for the needy
Occasional fellowship meals
Annual revival—to invite other churches in Presbytery to attend
The showing of slides on Liberia
A visit of a handbell choir from a church in the presbytery

At the end of the year the session and congregation evaluated the plan to see how well it did. It continued over the period of the pastorate with modifications and additions. When the pastor resigned one of the elders said: "You led us." That was full of meaning.

This report on Evergreen Church suggests that though a church be small, with leadership it can make progress.

Since there is a difference between small and large churches, administrators need to recognize the different kind of administration and program needed. In the section *For Further Thought and Study* will be found recommendations for further study in administration in a small church.

The second model will be called County Seat Church. The pastor was there for several years. It had a membership of around two hundred (200). Services were held every Sunday. The pastor lived in the manse. A fairly full and well-balanced program was in place. We will describe the planning process.

With the understanding that the program of the church belongs to the people, and that it had to be planned and not just allowed to happen, the session appointed a program planning committee each fall to plan for the year to come. It was made up of representatives from all the boards and committees, elders, deacons, CPW, youth and children's departments, and a few people representing the congregation. There were about 25 in all. A chairman was appointed by the session.

The pastor invited the various committees and boards to send in recommendation for next year and he included some from himself. These were compiled and mailed to each member of the committee.

The chairman of the committee met with the pastor to receive directions and information. The committee met about three times as a whole. It usually appointed subcommittees to do some of the work and report to the larger committee. The pastor did not meet with them. This was the opportunity the church had to make its own program in the absence of their minister. Often they counseled with the pastor in the meantime.

The committee submitted a report to the session, with the chairman meeting with them to lead the discussion. The pastor moderated the meeting.

The session presented the proposed program, after any revisions they made, to the Loyalty Dinner to which all members were invited. They formed small groups to discuss it. These reported to the meeting as a whole. All this was reported to the session for final action. The finished product then was mailed to all church members as a guide for the next year's program.

The pastor and session made assignments to the various boards and committees (or the assignments were automatically assumed) through whom the program was administered. The pastor and session assumed responsibility for over all administration. The program was coordinated through the church office with the help of the church secretary. The pastor supervised the process.

Let it be said again that these models are not presented as complete and perfect, but only as illustrations of some of the ways of planning and administering. There are many modifications of these ideas used in various congregations.

We said above that administration had to do with leading. We gave some suggestions concerning the pastor as leader. Now we take a brief look at lay leaders in the congregation. The success of the church's program depends upon many lay leaders who are called upon to serve in many capacities. The church could not function without them.

Because of their importance, we must be careful in the type of persons we select and the manner in which we choose them. The following guide might be helpful. Although it has been prepared more specifically for enlisting church school leaders and teachers, it can apply generally to all leaders.

ENLISTING AND TRAINING LEADERS

What standards do you use in selecting leaders? Here are some suggestions:

1. Is the person a member of the church? Your local congregation?
2. Is the person a growing Christian?
3. Is the person a regular attendant at worship and a participant in the life of the congregation?
4. Is the person apt to learn and to teach? (Not all people can teach.)
5. Is the person adequately educated for teaching?
6. Does the person have the capacity for relating to the persons and group she/he will be leading?
7. Is the person willing to take training for the task of leading?
8. Will the person commit himself or herself to the task for a specified time adequate for establishing a teaching-learning relationship?

What motives will you use in enlisting persons for leading? (Never call for volunteers. People need to be evaluated and chosen for particular jobs and tasks so they will be fitted to do them.)

1. You are wanted. We want you. You are the one we want. We think you can do what needs to be done at this particular time with this particular group.
2. You are needed. There is a need for what you have to offer. We think no one else will do what you can do here and now.
3. You can serve. Here is an opportunity for you to make a significant contribution to the life and growth of these persons. You can fill a need in the lives of these persons for Christian values and experience. What could be more valuable?
4. We will give you adequate space, materials and equipment to do the job.
5. We will give you some special training for the task.
6. We will negotiate with you for a specific amount of time that suits your availability rather than asking you to serve indefinitely.
7. We believe this will give you an opportunity to learn and grow and fulfill your desire to be needed and wanted. You will get satisfaction.
8. Could you consider this invitation a call from God to serve at this particular time and place.

NOTE: Pastors may need help from others to enlist leaders. They will need many to help train workers.

FOR FURTHER READING AND STUDY

The First Parish, J. Keith Cook, Westminster, 154 pages.

Read especially pages 25-27 and pages 51-71. These sections deal with leadership and administration.

Entering the World of the Small Church, Anthony G. Pappas, Alban Institute, 93 pages.

This is a must for those who want to understand how to work in the small church. Read especially Chapter IV "The Feel of Leadership: Understandings and Attitudes for Effective Leadership in the Small Church" and Chapter V "Leadership Activities in the Small Church World."

Keep alert to articles in *The Cumberland Presbyterian* and *The Missionary Messenger* on leadership and administration. For instance, "The Vision Beyond the Immediate Future," Lyle Schaller, issue of January 1992, *The Missionary Messenger.*

CHAPTER 10

The Pastor in Other Roles

THE PASTOR AS COUNSELOR

We pastors will be used as counselors by those who come to know and trust us. This may flatter our egos. The very idea that people think we are intelligent enough to help them with their problems! It makes us feel important. It is indeed a high compliment and a great trust.

Pastors occupy a special place in the community and in the lives of church members. They tend to think we are something special. They often accredit us with a professionalism we do not merit. They tend to think we know more than we actually know, and possess skills we have yet to acquire. So they bring their problems to us. They will talk with pastors about things they would never share with anyone else.

A word of caution to all of us, and especially to inexperienced ministers, is in order. We should move cautiously into this kind of ministry. It is highly complicated. Only a well trained person can deal with many of the concerns brought to us. There are some matters that anyone with intelligence, love and a little training can handle. There are more of the other kind.

Here are some suggestions which may help us fulfill more adequately this role of counselor.

First, *it is essential for us to receive more training in counseling before we let ourselves get too deeply involved in it.* We may need to read deeply in the field, be coached by a professional, or get more formal training in it.

In one town which had limited mental health services, a number of people in the ministry and helping professions were being called upon for counseling. A wide range of needs were represented in those who came for help. It was decided to secure the services of a psychologist to teach the counselors. A plan was set up whereby he came to their community every Saturday to give hours of instruction to them. Over several months they acquired nine hours of credit in psychology. This equipped them better to perceive the kinds of psychological problems people had; how, to whom and when to refer; and how to deal with other personal and family concerns. They did not feel they had become professionals in such a short time, but they were better able to avoid mistakes and to be more secure in what they were doing.

Second, *there are books being published in this field which will enlighten us*. We need to keep abreast by reading them. Experienced counselors can advise us about the best books to purchase.

Third, *refer some persons to able professionals*. Psychotic and neurotic persons often come to pastors for help. They have little understanding of themselves. We need to be able to know how to determine the kinds of conditions we are dealing with and to let well established professionals care for extreme cases. There are, however, some problems we can deal with which are of a pastoral and religious nature. For those who are somewhat inexperienced, some words of guidance may help in avoiding pitfalls right now. Here are a few.

Fourth, *Some dos and don'ts in counseling*.

a. *Avoid giving advice and providing answers*.

It is easy to take the line of least resistance and satisfy people with immediate answers or opinions. It can backfire on us and cease to be helpful in the long run. The best approach is to attempt to lead them to understand the problems they face, suggest sources of help, and encourage them to find their own answers. Often after talking with a counselor some come to see a way out on their own. What they needed was a good sounding board.

b. *Learn to listen*.

Listening is an art. It has to be learned. We ministers tend to talk more than we listen. We are victims of an assumption that we have *the* word people need. We are also entrapped with the idea that being called to the ministry has given us some unusual wisdom not enjoyed by ordinary human beings. Better be careful here. Human pride flourishes in this kind of thinking. So—listen more than you talk.[1]

c. *Practice confidentiality*.

Keep confidential the names of persons whom you are counseling. Don't share with *anyone* what goes on in counseling sessions without the consent of the counselee.

Don't use illustrations in sermons of problems which have been dealt with in counseling sessions. This is betrayal and threatens people who have trusted us. Only a very insensitive person would do this. Parishioners must know they can trust us beyond a shadow of a doubt.

Ask for consent of the counselees before getting help and information on their problems from doctors, psychologists or psychiatrists.

Take great care not to share names and information about counselees with other professional persons unless it is approved by them.

Confidentiality extends even to cases in court. Whatever is told a counselor is privileged information. We do not have to divulge it.

Don't joke about and share counselee's problems with other ministers. Sometimes less thoughtful counselors do this. It is unprofessional and unchristian.

Don't carry gossip. Some ministers make trouble because they do. Be careful

---

[1] *One Listening to Another*, Douglas V. Steere, Harper, 1955, may be out of print, but is an excellent primer on listening.

about evaluating lay people before other lay persons, when a group is selecting leaders. Set an example for the session and committee members about keeping in confidence what the group decides should be kept quiet. Don't leak information.

d. *Keep the relationship with the counselee on a professional level.*

If we do counseling with a particular person of the opposite sex over a period of weeks or months it is possible that the counselee will develop feelings for the counselor akin to "falling in love." If this problem cannot be worked through or if the counselor begins to reciprocate such feelings the relationship should be modified or ended. The counselee may be referred to another counselor. This kind of relationship does not always occur. The main point here is that, as counselors, we are relating professionally to a counselee. Perhaps this is another caution to make us aware that counseling is a professional job which requires training and experience.

e. *Set limits on counseling sessions.*

Allow time (a week?) between counseling sessions, and have a mutual agreement with the counselee on the amount of time to be used in each session. Thirty minutes to an hour are suggested. After a number of sessions, plans should be made to terminate the sessions at a reasonable date. This is to say that sessions should not be prolonged indefinitely, however they should continue as long as needed.

Unless some discipline is exercised, some counselees will overuse their privilege. It is important that pastors guard their time and learn how to use it in such a way as to accomodate as many persons as possible and not spend too much of it with a few.

f. *Do counseling in a setting where other persons are in the building.*

Although this word seems to contradict what has been said about confidentiality, it is wise to follow it. Whereas the sessions will be private they should be held in a place which will not be inducive to gossip. Pastors must safeguard the reputations of the persons involved, and prevent compromising situations to arise. This applies more specifically to counseling of persons of the opposite sex.

g. *As a rule, it is best for families of counselees to know they are seeing a counselor.*

The consent and support of the family are important. In some cases a wife, a husband, a son, or a daughter may wish to keep the fact a secret. This is understandable. However, not to let the family know is to run risks that could lead to trouble. There may be good exceptions to this rule, but they should be considered very seriously.

h. *Do not encourage touching in a counseling relationship.* Counselees are often very vulnerable emotionally, and can misinterpret intentions and be easily influenced or misused. Treat them with care and reverence.

i. *Some counseling is supervision of workers.*

Pastors are often called upon to train people to lead, teach, plan and serve in many ways. This is a part of their role. They should be alert to any indication

> **FOR FURTHER READING ABOUT THE PASTOR AND COUNSELING**
>
> *Family Therapy in Pastoral Ministry*, J. C. Wynn, Harper & Row, 1982
>
> *The Christian Shepherd*, Seward Hiltner, Abingdon, 1954. This older book is still useful and contains valuable material.
>
> *Loving Each Other*, A Challenge of Human Relationships, Leo F. Buscaglia, Fawcett, 1984
>
> See also "Resources for Ministry," Dr. Roy W. Hall, issue of August 1990, *The Cumberland Presbyterian*; "Stepping Together," E. C. Hurley, issue of April 1990; and "Depression," George Nichols, MD, issue of December 1990.

that any one person is coming too often for such help. There may be secondary reasons for such visits.

The suggestions above may appear to encourage suspicion and extreme caution on the part of pastors. They are not intended as such. They are alerts for the inexperienced to save them from common pitfalls, while at the same time giving them essential guidance.

Fifth, *family counseling is intricate and demanding*. It calls for a lot of knowledge and understanding of the family as a system and as a set of complex relationships. Be careful in doing it. Remember we need training to avoid mistakes and to become efficient.

Perhaps these brief and simple guidelines will save us a lot of trouble and lead us further toward learning how to be a helpful and healing counselor.

THE PASTOR AS THEOLOGIAN

The word *theology* derives from the Greek words THEOS, meaning God; and LOGOS, meaning discourse. The English word *theo* means God and *logy* means science, doctrine or theory.

Theology is defined as the study of God and the relations between God and universe; the study of religious doctrines and matters of divinity; a special system of the study as held by a particular religion or denomination.

Theology has been referred to as the queen of the sciences.

A theologian is a student of or authority on theology or a theology. It is essential to a fruitful and sound ministry that we be theologians. The pastor as theologian is not mentioned in the *Confession of Faith* because it is not a Biblical word, however it is assumed without question that we are to fill this role. There could be no ministry without it.

In fact, ministers and lay persons alike are theologians whether we think of ourselves in this way or not. The first time we began to ask questions about God we became theologians. That begins early, especially in Christian homes. We all have some degree of knowledge of theology. We either were taught it formally in the home, or we absorbed it. We continued our learning at church school and worship; and in the various settings and relationships in the church as a whole. We deal with it in teaching, preaching, worship and all other activities related to our faith.

Its importance insists that we become students and continue throughout our lives to increase our knowledge of it, to evaluate it, and to keep up with current trends in the field. Our role as theologians is basic to our ministry.

Theology is based on scripture. Scripture is the record of the revelation of God to humankind. God was revealed to human beings through their total lives over many centuries covering the gamut of events; therefore, there is no experience to which the scriptures do not speak. We search the scriptures to get a knowledge of God. In them we learn of God's nature, purpose, will and intention for us, and to see how God acts and why.

We believe that what the Bible tells us of God is verified in our lives and those of all other human beings. How often have we come to affirm that the God of scripture is the Lord who lives and guides our lives today! In cases where experience does not confirm what the Bible says, we live by faith, which is assurance.

As theologians into whom God has put a yearning to know and trust, we continue to search the scriptures to know more about the ultimate source of our being, and our destiny.

Some have been led to write books of theology which guide and stimulate our thinking. They record what others have come to think and believe. They reflect many viewpoints. We consider them all. As we continue to explore, we affirm what we have come to believe; but we do not close our minds to future revelations.

Life and thought never stay the same. God continues to work in the hearts and lives of people. Human beings continue to change and to learn. New situations call for revised attitudes and insights. New theological trends emerge and we have to become aware of and informed about them if we keep in communications with the people of our times.

We are grateful to the great theologians, and the lesser ones, through whom God has spoken. Beginning with Paul, we can name others such as Augustine, Thomas Aquinas, Martin Luther, John Calvin, John Knox, John Wesley, Finis Ewing, Robert Donnell, Karl Barth, Paul Tillich, Emil Brunner, Reinhold and Richard Niebuhr, Dietrich Bonhoeffer, and countless others.

We do not accept unequivocally what any theologian says without first examining it in the light of scripture, for scripture is "the infallible rule of faith and practice, the authoritative guide for Christian living."

We seek God for ourselves, though using the help of others, for our faith must issue from the fires of our own experience, and be hammered out on the anvil of our daily lives as we "work out our own salvation with fear and trembling."

As beginning ministers who are to become faithful theologians "rightfully dividing the word of truth," and learning "sound doctrine," where can we find resources which will mature and guide our thinking? Here are some suggestions for starters.

Begin simply with only a few books. Start with the *Confession of Faith*.

Read *What Cumberland Presbyterians Believe*, E. K. Reagin.

Broaden out by reading *Christian Doctrine*, Shirley C. Guthrie, Jr. This is a larger book and will require time and thought.

You need a book or two to introduce you to trends and schools of thought in theology. For this why not read *Winds of Doctrine*, Thomas H. Campbell?

Further, *Contemporary American Theologies*, Deane William Ferm, 1981, and 1990 will pitch you head first into the whirlpool of theological trends of our day. It is a difficult book to read, but it will give you essential perspective and knowledge.

For helping you understand the meaning of theological words purchase *A Theological Word Book of the Bible*, Alan Richardson.

All these can be purchased through the Cumberland Presbyterian Resource Center, 1978 Union Avenue, Memphis, TN 38104.

THE PASTOR AS PRESBYTER

In the *Confession of Faith*, the Constitution (section 2.62, page 30) lists among scriptural role of ministry "Elder or presbyter—who shares in the leadership and government of the church."

We are a connectional church. There is an interrelatedness between the session, presbytery, synod and general assembly. We are a whole with different parts. Ministers sometimes act as if they are not subject to the presbytery; and churches, at times, neglect the actions and directives of the governing bodies. They speak of presbytery, synod and general assembly as "they" and "them," rather than "we" and "us."

Ours is a representative form of government with elders and ministers comprising the judicatories. This means we have a part in decision making. In other words, we rule ourselves. We do not have a bishop or superintendent over us. The power of the church is vested in the people and their representatives.

Therefore, we have obligations. We are to comply with the actions of the judicatories. As ministers and elders, we are to be willing to serve as representatives to the various church courts, to accept membership on boards and committees, to attend meetings of these bodies, and to discharge faithfully what we promised to do when we were ordained. This is more than a duty. It is a privilege; and fulfills our own nature as a connectional church.

> **FOR FURTHER READING ABOUT THE PASTOR AS PRESBYTER**
>
> Read the Constitution of the Cumberland Presbyterian Church in the *Confession of Faith*. Memorize as much of it as you can.
> If you have not done so, read "Why Go To Presbytery?" by Howard Walton in the August 1991 issue of *The Cumberland Presbyterian*.

When we joined the congregation, we joined the whole church. If we have never participated on the various levels and have limited our activity to the local church, we have yet to experience what the whole church is and what it does. We affirm these functions in spite of the fact that meetings of church judicatories can be time consuming, boring and terribly frustrating, as well as fulfilling. Dispel from your mind right now the idea that serving the Lord is *always* inspirational! Service entails discipline and sweat as well as joy.

Representing the church as an elder often means getting off the job, finding a replacement, forfeiting salary, giving thought and time, and spending energy and effort. The same can be said in part for the ministers. They are busy with pastoral work and have many other tasks to perform, yet, a vital part of their role is to serve as a presbyter.

There are rewards. By serving the whole church we come to a sense of belonging, of being a part of a wider fellowship. We make new friends and enrich each others' lives. We enter a wider field of usefulness and catch a vision of world mission. Together we feel we are making a difference on the earth.

THE PASTOR IN RELATION TO THE COMMUNITY

A basic assumption for ministry is that pastors are members of the community where we serve and are responsible first of all, for being good citizens. We are obligated to contribute to its growth and betterment.

It is important for us to think of ourselves as *permanent* citizens, not transients. We are to sink our roots there as if we will never move.

Unfortunately, attitudes and practices make it difficult for us to think or act like this. The average pastorate extends over only a few years. Pastors move in and move out, just as large numbers of lay persons do. People tend to think of us as short-time residents. We are lumped by the old-timers into the category of newcomers. That gives us little or no status.

There is also the matter of becoming accepted. In a city the basic problem is trying to become known and to escape the status of a number. In communities which are smaller and more provincial, acceptance is hard to come by. People come to know us fairly soon. Acceptance is another matter. They will be nice and friendly, but if we happen to get too close to community skeletons and sacred traditions, they treat us like outsiders. Some things are none of your business; not yet, if ever.

One pastor remembers, after having been in the community for seven years, that someone said to him, "Well, you are one of us." When this was made know to another citizen of long standing, he said, "That was one of those liberals speaking!" Though said in evident jest, it reflected something real.

Regardless of these factors, we will have greater success fitting into a community if we have a citizenship mentality rather than a transient mentality. Thinking and acting as permanent citizens hastens acceptance and appreciation.

When Henry M. moved to *Our Town* and began what turned out to be a long pastorate, he decided he would be a citizen first of all; that is, he thought of himself basically as a member of the community, not just the pastor of a congregation. This was really radical thinking for him. He had never done this before.

He did not want to belong just to the Cumberland Presbyterians. He wanted to belong to everyone. He knew who paid his salary and who had called him, and intended to fulfill his obligations; but his image of himself went far beyond being a pastor of that congregation. Fortunately, the people of the church wanted a pastor to act like a full-fledged citizen so it worked out pretty well.

He had already had some experience in ecumenicity and was not sectarian. Building on this, he developed an interest and concern for all churches, not just his own. So, in a sense he belonged to all congregations and all Christian people in *Our Town*. He owed something to the unchurched too, but he was not sure just what he could do about that at present. His attitude really opened the door to an interesting pastorate.

Although he was committed to minister to his congregation, and to help it fulfill its ministry, he worked hard on his attitude toward the growth of other churches. If indeed he belonged to all churches he would want all churches to grow. Being human, he hoped they would not grow any faster than his. He would not have claimed that he had arrived at a perfect attitude about all churches, but he did make progress in that direction and worked hard on seeing the whole and not just the particular.

It was an engaging venture of growth in vision and ecumenicity; for he was moving in the direction of an attitude which would express itself in believing that what happened in other churches was just as important as what was happening in his. It almost caused him trouble when he occasionally advised some newcomers to consider another church than his own because he thought they could serve the Lord better there. Some of his members thought he was being foolish when they needed so badly all the givers they could get to help meet the budget!

A part of his cooperative attitude was affirmed in his becoming active in the ministerial association and trying to relate to others who did not belong. Also, there were a lot of good things being done in the community through the Department of Human Resources, the Mental Health Association, The Association for Retarded

Children, the Council on Aging, and other groups. He began to work in some of these organizations as time permitted. It opened the way to a wider ministry. It did not necessarily add members to his congregation.

So much for what one pastor tried to do in becoming a part of a community. Henry M. is a composite of many ministers, some of whom did even more than he. His attitude however, is what is important. Some in *Our Town* assumed wider perspectives because of him.

But there is more. Much, much more! How does a minister relate to the power structure of a community and deal with some entrenched evils? Ah! Better be careful here Henry M.! *Our Town* does not like meddlers, especially if they are newcomers of either long or short-time duration.

In every community there are the ins and outs, the privileged and unprivileged, the poor and the rich, the accepted and the rejected. Attitudes and practices are well set. If pastors depart from what is customary they run the risk of rejection, criticism, ostracism and other forms of hostility. If they do not act with wisdom they also run the risk of making their ministry ineffective. There is a tight line to walk.

Every city, town, or village has its own power structure and pecking order. Old-timers do their best to maintain this. They run for office and get elected as long as they can, and they despise and fear newcomers who challenge the status quo. If pastors and other concerned citizens challenge some of the social injustices in the community or what is called good business practices, they run counter to these keepers of traditions and preservers of power. They have labels to put on those who "do not like our town," and know how to use them devastatingly. Social and racial walls, unseen though they are in many cases, remain intact and crumble slowly. Practices maintain themselves even though many of them virtually enslave members in the community.

Sincere pastors with sensitive social consciences want to get involved in change. They want to be change agents. They not only want to speak as prophets, but they want to act as prophets. A dangerous role, and almost an impossible one for pastors of conservative institutions. For when a man becomes a part of a church he is a part of the accepted ways of the community, a part of the "better people" who often bless the status quo, blindly or cynically. Churches usually have representatives of the power structure in their membership. How can a pastor be a change agent in the community in the light of this kind of mixture? How can one maintain one's acceptance and try to make changes without being run out of town or just marked off as being a radical or a clown? There are those who manage to do it. Blessings upon them!

It is difficult to bring about in society what the gospel says ought to be. Too many of us are unwilling to try. Not many of us have worked out a way to express social concern in the pastoral ministry. Part of the blame lies in our lack of training for it. Most denominations train ministers to take care of the churchly functions of ministry without equipping us to relate the gospel redemptively to the community in which ministry is to be done. Few of us have acquired nerve or skills for this. There are many who wisely enter into the long pull, patiently waiting and working to open doors and not becoming aggressive too quickly.

Time and space forbid our going further with this concern but we do want to establish the fact that we cannot claim to be ministers without somehow relating the gospel to the world of injustice and inequality because human beings are affected. Unacceptable living conditions for many exist everywhere. How can we preach personal salvation without adding the dimension of social responsibility and witness? How can we be silent when people are hurting?

In spite of the rationalizations for poverty, injustice and inequality we hear so often, there are good reasons for making the gospel socially relevant. Let us consider these questions:

> How can we minister to individuals without coming to understand and try to improve the social setting in which persons are either nurtured toward wholeness or victimized and destroyed?
>
> Must we not take into account the radical differences in the quality of life in which persons exist in our society? Do we blame the individuals altogether, or take another look at our systems?
>
> Do we believe that society is so resistant to change that it cannot occur? Or do we believe that changes can be made and they can be made by people who decide to make them?
>
> Should not the whole community be so structured and operated that the grace of God can be mediated to all people? Should not the grace of God be expressed in community life? Do not all people deserve to receive the blessings of God? Why else did Christ pray "Thy kingdom come?"[2]

We are dealing with deeply controversial matters here. Those who read these pages may disagree with what has been said. That is understandable. But does not loving God with our whole being and loving our neighbor as ourselves lead us to follow as far as they take us? Do they not lead us to Christian action on behalf of a large percentage of people for whom our system has not provided well, while making others excessively rich?

We are not advocating a plan for the reconstruction of society. No one has ever been able to do that effectively. It is a part of the sinfulness of the human race. Let me as the writer say a personal word. Over most of my ministry I have been troubled with this problem of applying the gospel to society. I have never found for myself a satisfying way to do it. Others seem to have and I have great respect for them. But regardless of not having found a satisfying way to express myself in this regard, I have carried a deep and troubling concern for the millions in our world who are victims of unjust systems. I am convinced that the gospel speaks to them and calls us to try to apply it to the whole of life. I want to make some suggestions of what you can do in this matter. These come out of my own ministry. They may seem tame and ineffective but they at least suggest a place to begin if you want to move in this direction.

A word of caution first. When we consider how to relate the gospel to society we are faced with a highly complicated and deeply entrenched concern. It is controversial and people can be disturbed quickly about it, or by what we may say. It is not something for a novice to deal with. It requires thought and study not only of theology but of sociology. So prepare yourself. In some communities relations are so personal that any criticism or suggestion will be taken personally. Also, time is essential for anyone to become informed about conditions in any community.

---

[2] "Get Your Feet Wet" Haskell M. Miller, *Circuit Rider*, UME publishing House, May 1988, was the source for some of ideas in this section.

Perhaps a good first goal is to try to sensitize the consciences of people. You can do that by talking about the problems. This can be done with individuals, in private conversations, through sermons and discussions, leaving an openness so people will have a chance to express their views. Such dialog can be productive.

We do not have to preach whole sermons on the topics. There are illustrations and thrusts which can be done in sermons from time to time.

We have to follow our own feelings in these matters. If we are too uncomfortable and unsure in dealing with them, we ought to proceed slowly. Basically, it is essential for us to develop our own theology and philosophy about the social application of the gospel. Don't think we have to copy someone else, or let them push us into something we are not ready to enter. Re-read the life and teachings of Jesus and try to hear with new ears what he says that has to do with the needs of all people.

As you see, these are only brief and incomplete suggestions, intended only as starters. Perhaps what has been said has issued more challenges than can be answered, and calls for more information and courage than most of us have. But we cannot talk about Christian ministry without talking about the kind of world we live in and what we can and ought to do about it.

Every time we pray the Lord's Prayer we say—"Thy kingdom come, thy will be done in earth as it is in heaven." That is asking for a world in which there is justice and equality, is it not? We are praying with Jesus that it will come. He believed it would come and prayed for its coming. But more, he gave his life to bring it. Can we enter into this part of his ministry?

Let's turn now to consider another matter concerning our relationship to the place we serve. In spite of the fact that we may ignore some things about the community we move into, there are some things we look for. If there are children, we want to find out first about the educational system. We look also for a lively community; one that is growing and in which good things are happening. As time goes by, we may become disappointed and grow restless and want to move. It is easy to think the next community will be better. Unconsciously we may be looking for a perfect place, as if any existed.

> **FOR FURTHER READING ABOUT THE PASTOR AND COMMUNITY**
>
> *Building Effective Ministry, Theory and Practice in the Local Church*, Edited Carl F. Dudley, Harper & Row, 1983, 267 pages. This book deals with many matters, among which is the relation of church and community.
>
> ❖ To what extent can you apply the principles in this section to your present church situation?

One pastor who became very dissatisfied with the small city in which he lived, with the help of his wife, did some soul searching about his attitude. He reviewed the place and reevaluated the opportunities for service. There were many, if not always the kind he had dreamed of giving. He considered his alternatives. He began to think again about his philosophy of ministry in relation to where it should be done. He came up with some thoughts that helped him. They may or may not be for everyone but they opened a door for him. We share them here.

> Every community is a microcosm of the world with many of the elements of the cosmos in it; it is a microcosm of all places with most of the elements of all places in it.

No community will have everything fully and in balance as some others. But every community has assets and liabilities.

If one thinks of ambition, some places offer greater opportunities for a ministry that will build status and attract attention. If one thinks of service, every community has many opportunities for it, though they may not be what was desired at first. But every place is representative of every other place, and has its own uniqueness.

So—if this is true, each community is as important as any other in the world, no matter the size or location. What one does in one is as worthy as what may be done in another. There is no rank in service. However, because of the human condition, rank is still placed high on the list. All of us want to shine, and it is so nice to shine brighter than anyone else!

To put this attitude of equal value of all communities into practice means to recognize that the perfect place for service is not to be found. There are opened and closed doors everywhere. Knowing this we try to create a ministry wherever we are, the nature and need of the community, our sensitiveness, what we have to offer and the leadership of the Holy Spirit determining what it will be.

If this is done, there results a peace of mind, a freeing of the spirit, and a satisfaction which prevent our seeing greener grass on the other side of the fence.

Well, you may not buy into this for yourself, but it saved one pastor's ministry.

Although much more can be said about the pastor's relation to the community, perhaps this is enough to set the course of your thinking about it.

THE PASTOR AND MINISTERIAL ETHICS

Ethics have to do with standards of conduct, and moral judgments. They deal with right and wrong. They call for decisions. These decisions have to be based on something solid and true. For the Christian this includes the Ten Commandments, the life and teachings of Jesus, the principle of love, the leadership of the Holy Spirit, and a sense of responsibility.

Taking these as guides we have to make decisions in the midst of varying situations. Situations should not be the final determining factors in choices, but they do have to be taken into consideration.

Ministers are set into the midst of responsible relationships. They assume roles they are to fulfill. What is to guide them ethically as they carry on the work of ministry?

The scope of this book as an introduction to ministry, and time and space limitations, prevent our going into depth regarding ministerial ethics, or how one arrives at certain decisions concerning them. Rather, we will be introduced to brief guidelines for helping ministers do what is morally and ethically right. These will seem incomplete, but at the same time helpful to the beginning and inexperienced candidate or pastor. They are practical and brief. They appear to be rules, but are meant as suggestions to chart the way through potentially dangerous and confusing situations. They are not listed in any order and do not follow a logical pattern. Take them for what they are, but take them seriously.

Stay away from where you have been pastor. Once you break the pastoral relationship with a congregation, you are no longer their leader. Don't meddle with what is going on and don't criticize your successor. Turn it over to him or her. It is no longer your church. It is under the responsibility of someone else. If you do visit any members or are asked to do funerals or weddings, do so only after consulting with the present pastor.

Keep your promises not to share confidences. Ministers must learn to carry many secrets and burdens which cannot be shared with anyone. Don't let the devil of gossip and the human love of the lurid and unusual cause you to be a traitor. Swallow that yen to tell juicy, mouth-watering bits about human behavior. Grow up and act like a professional rather than an amateur. This is hard for certain personalities to handle. If it is a problem for you, go see a counselor for help. A great deal is at stake here. It may be someone'e reputation and happiness.

Live a chaste life and be true to your wedding vows. Ministers are given much freedom. They come and go freely into homes and associate easily with many different people. Occasions do arise in which they can go astray. Stay away from situations which invite or make possible that which is forbidden. Don't be afraid to run.

Pay your debts. Perhaps in recent years with better salaries, ministers do not have the difficulty they once had paying their bills. It is essential that ministers not over-spend or let their families create financial problems. Honesty is a basic virtue. Maturity in money matters is a must for ministers.

Don't gossip about former pastors. Don't gossip at all. How can we help it? Most of us slip occasionally. There are always those persons in a congregation who want to put down a former minister for one reason or another. Don't play into their hands. If they will gossip about one, they will do so about another, including you. Understand what gossip is. It is an effort to build yourself up at the expense of another person. Be bigger than that. Insecure and sick people seem to thrive on it. Help heal them.

Give a good day's work. Ministers are largely unsupervised. They have to be self-starters and maintainers or they will loaf on the job. There is no place for a lazy preacher, and though the people may tolerate them, they loathe them.

Don't dig present or former members for money. Some ministers are con artists. They know how to get things from their parishioners. People are soft toward ministers. The bamboozler knows how to take advantage of them and appear to be loving and kind at the same time, so much in need and ever so grateful. Unfortunately many members are vulnerable and never learn. Others grow cynical. If you persist as a money grubber, it will catch up with you sooner or later—we hope!

Enter into the former pastor's ministry. Don't junk it all!. Some pastors move into a new congregation and act as if there had never been any other minister there. They wipe the slate clean of all programs and begin new ones. There is no continuation of former ministry or traditional practices. This is ethically wrong and very hurtful to the former pastor. It is also foolish. There are always some, and often many, good things former leaders have established. They worked hard to get them accepted. The people are familiar with them and have responded to them. Why destroy them? Unless your ego dictates it. Most ministers do have ego problems and need help with them. Sometimes they have bad images of themselves and a successful program of a former pastor is a threat to them. We may need some help from understanding counselors in managing such problems.

Don't exaggerate your successes or lie about your education. Let people find out about your successes without your telling them. It is better this way. Success is always relative anyway. Also, if you have succeeded tell God about it and keep the people in the dark. God does not mind being bored but the people hate it. People are not always interested in diplomas, though they want a capable person to serve them. They probably evaluate you by the job you do. This is not to discourage education. It is to counsel honesty and humility.

Don't compete with ministers of other churches of any denomination. They are team members. All Christians and Christian ministers are working in the same vineyard. Although we are divided into denominations, none of us has all the truth or is the best. It takes all of us to make something whole. Naturally, we want our particular congregation to grow, and humanly speaking, we like to get ahead. The disciples showed some of these tendencies but were reprimanded by Jesus. We are an ecumenical denomination. We think we are all in the same boat. What benefits one, helps others. Jesus prayed that we would be one as a witness of the faith, "That they all may be one...so that the world may believe...." (John 17:21).

Don't steal sheep. If others seem to be happily secure in another fold why bother them? Do we think our particular brand of religion is better and that our church can minister more fully? It may be. That is not the point. Get out and find your own sheep. Don't let someone else do your evangelism for you. This does not mean we will reject any who seem to want to move into our congregation. If we want to be ethical we will be careful not to initiate or encourage people to leave other congregations in favor of our own. There are those who probably are ready for membership in your group. Let the initiative for the move be their own.

> **FOR FURTHER READING ABOUT MINISTERIAL ETHICS**
>
> *In Response to God,* Isabel Rogers, CLC Press, 1969, a Covenant Life Curriculum book. 350 pages.
> *Christian Ethics,* David H.C. Read, J.B. Lippincott Company, 1969. 125 pages.
> *Who Sets the Standards? Behavior, Society, and the Church,* Haskell M. Miller, The Pilgrim Press, 1989, 173 pages.

Don't flatter people. We are all suckers for compliments and strokes. All of us need words of encouragement. There is a legitimate place for stroking and complimenting, as long as it is not a gimmick used to influence people. It can become a cheap PR trick.

Keep your word. We earn respect and authority through credibility. Be careful of what you promise; be true in keeping your promises. It does not take many failures for people to find you out. It is then your leadership becomes nil.

Don't use people for your own purposes. Self-serving pastors learn how to manipulate members to achieve their own particular goals. To use persons for ulterior purposes is to make something less than human beings out of them. Do you remember having been manipulated by someone without recognizing it until later? How did you feel? There's nothing more devastating than to realize you've been had! It takes a long time, if ever, to forget the persons involved.

Don't set elders against deacons, or vice versa, to get your own way. We are using negatives in these statements because we know that some of these means have been used for selfish ends. We need some strong "no-nos" to put a stop to it. Pray God will give you grace and integrity enough to prevent your ever setting groups in the church against each other to achieve your aims.

Don't use a call to another church to get a raise. Yes, this has been done. How cheap can you get?

Be meticulous in handling church money. Keep records. Better still, let others do it. It is the business of lay members. If for some reason you may handle a fund of any kind, share the task with someone else and report regularly. Have the accounts examined.

Deal above board with the session. Don't caucus with a few to get your programs over. Try to influence session members from doing this. It makes for disruption. It is not fair. Neither is it ethical or Christian. Keep everything out in the open and let everyone know what the score is. This builds unity.

Use everyone who is qualified on church boards and committees, not just your cronies. It is easy to favor some over others. After all, the pastor is human and has personal likes and dislikes. It is difficult to be fair. But we had better be fair, in all things, big and little. It is a matter of Christian witness.

Inform your church monthly on matters of finance. Don't cache funds away in secret bank accounts as some churches do. The officials fear if the people know money is on hand, they will not continue to give. But the people give the money. They deserve to know the financial status of the congregation. This builds trust and trust is essential to a healthy church.

CONCLUSION

No one can ever adequately do the work of Christian ministry. The task is too great. We do not have all the skills essential to the whole ministry. More needs call for attention than we can ever fill. We cannot see all the people who need us. We cannot lead the church into all the services it should give. No day, no pastorate and no life time is long enough. So we are apt to be overwhelmed with the largeness of the task.

As a beginning minister we may need to take another look at our calling. If we are serving a small church or churches, the load may not appear to be as heavy as the roles indicate. As we grow more experienced and assume larger churches or parishes, the load will increase. If we are a tentmaker and have to work at a secular job and hold a church or churches also, we can immediately see the bigness of the job, and seek ways of getting it done better.

In any case, we need to think about how we can do all that needs to be done. Here are a few suggestions which may help.

1. *Delegate tasks and responsibilities.* Good leaders do this. Learn to use lay persons as much as possible. Enlist them and help prepare them. Explain fully what the task requires. Write a job description. Provide materials and information. Give as much training as possible. Coach them and support them.

Lay persons are already doing much of the work, but probably more people can be enlisted and more assignments made. The following list suggests the things which might be delegated.

> Some special pastoral visiting
> Visitation of shut-ins, nursing homes, hospitals
> Doing office work, like preparing the bulletin and newsletter
> Helping direct Christian education
> Odd jobs often left to the pastor such as turning out lights, opening and closing

buildings, making arrangements for meetings, etc.
Caring for memorial gifts
Preparing descriptions and rules for the use of buildings
Teaching special classes
Doing Bible Study
And others.

2. *Make schedules.* Plan each day carefully and work your plan. Carry over to the next day what you did not get done. There will be interferences. Cut down on as many as possible. Set priorities and do what is essential, not just what is important. If you don't make schedules you will be the victim of whatever persons, events, calls, demands and problems invade your day. Even at best it is difficult to hold the line.

3. *Make time for devotions.* Put this at the top of your list. The Psalmist says we must be still in order to know God. We also need to be still in order to find strength. Our tendency is to rush into the day. Before we do this it is best to relax first. Don't rush into worship and prayer. Ease into it. Set a time for your daily devotions and keep it. Pressure often produces panic and frustration. These scramble our attitude and perspective. It is essential to relax and let go.

4. *Take time off weekly.* And take vacations. You will burn out if you don't. Take time to rest and do something different. It is good to have a hobby. It relaxes and renews. After time off you can come back refueled. If you are too busy to take time off, you are much too busy. The outcome of the Kingdom is not in our hands. It is in God's. You are not called to guarantee the success of the work of God. You are called to be faithful. Time taken off saves time in the long run.

5. *Think of yourself as an enabler.* Some ministers are hands on pastors. They want to do a little bit of everything and seem to feel they are the only ones who can do things right. The job of the minister is not to do all ministry, but to enable others to do it. We are called "to equip the saints for the work of ministry."

6. *Put daily and weekly work schedules and yearly events on the calendar.* This is more than planning for each day. Time should be set for study, visitation, meetings, and so forth. Ask the people to honor your schedule, especially your time for study and devotions. It should be understood what you are to do every day of the week, such as hours for study, hours for visiting, and hours for meetings. Plan for things to happen, don't just let them happen. Yearly events, planned by the entire church, should be set into the calendar. If people know what you are doing daily, weekly and if they know what is planned for the year, they can adapt their schedules accordingly.

7. *Get rid of the time killers.* Use the telephone wisely. Make calls instead of some visits if this is acceptable. Don't extend telephone calls. Don't allow others to do so. Learn to prevent long visits by drop-ins. Don't extend meetings beyond a useful time. Attend only the meetings that are necessary. Don't put off what can be done now. Don't try to do too much in any one morning, afternoon or evenings. Learn to say no.

We can learn as we become more experienced how to facilitate work to enable us to do more.

8. *Accept the fact that ministers' time is largely not their own,* and that our work weeks will range (in a full-time pastorate) from fifty-three to sixty-seven hours.

God has called us to a great and demanding vocation and we have responded.

We must keep on doing our best and learning how to do better, believing we can, with wise efforts and God's help, achieve what is essential to an effective ministry.

> "See that you fulfill the ministry which you have received from the Lord." (Col. 4:17)
>
> "We know that in everything God works for good with those who love him, who are called according to his purpose." (Rom. 8:38)
>
> "Having this ministry by the mercies of God, we do not lose heart." (I Cor. 4:1)
>
> "Looking to Jesus the pioneer and perfecter of our faith, who for the joy that was set before him endured the cross." (Heb. 12:2)

This Chapter ends the presentation of the roles for the ministry. There are ten of them. They do not exactly coincide with those given in he *Confession of Faith*, however they cover substantially the same responsibilities.

This has been an effort to present an introduction to the ministry for those who are beginning or those who are thinking about entering it. It has been also an attempt to acquaint lay persons with the meaning of ministry and to provide some guidelines as they participate in it, and to bring them to a better understanding of the work of the ordained clergy.

THE EPILOGUE
Symbols of a Unified Ministry

THE MINISTRY AS A TAPESTRY

The roles of ministry should not stand out separately as if they are not related to each other. To allow this is to split ourselves into different persons in doing it. Like being a pastor person at one time, a preacher person at another, a priestly person at still another, a teacher person at yet another, and so on.

On the other hand, if we view ministry as a tapestry we are making, its separate parts can be woven together into a unified pattern. We will weave the strands of the gospel, pastoral care, worship, teaching, evangelism and others into the pattern of love as needs arise.

The weaving is never complete but the beauty of the design emerges gradually as time goes by. When we look at it we do not see its separate threads but all the filaments woven into an integrated whole.

THE MINISTRY AS A MULTI-COLORED ROBE

The minister's robe is a symbol of the office of ministry. Black was used as the color for many years. Recently robes of various colors have appeared. Sometimes a robe will contain a number of shades.

Think of the many roles of ministry as so many hues. Blend them into the cloth subtly and let the multi-colored robe signify the unity of our ministry.

THE MINISTRY AS ONE HAT

Occasionally we hear a person say he wears many hats in his occupation. He means he has many functions. In that sense the minister has many hats. But for the minister to change hats as he moves from one function to another is to give emphasis to the separate roles rather than unity. Why not just one hat? And let it be blue. Blue is the color of loyalty and faithfulness. One hat—one ministry.

THE MINISTRY AS A CROSS

The Cross symbolizes the suffering ministry of Jesus Christ. It was one offering of love. The cross bars are like arms reaching out with compassion to everyone. One cross—one hope—one ministry.

THE MINISTRY AS A WHEEL

Perhaps the best symbol of ministry is a wheel with the spokes extending out from the hub. Each spoke signifies a role of service, the hub being Christ and his work in which we participate. Here is complete unity and symmetry. When the wheel was invented the human race rolled forward in a great spurt of progress. But nothing in comparison with the innovation of Christ and his ministry of love.

There is one body and one spirit, just as you were called to the one hope that belongs to your call, one Lord, one faith, one baptism, one God and Father of us all, who is above all and through all and in all.[1]

Amen.

---

[1] Ephesians 4:4-6

www.ingramcontent.com/pod-product-compliance
Lightning Source LLC
Chambersburg PA
CBHW080514110426
42742CB00017B/3110